Collins

EXPLORE ENGLISH

Student's Coursebook 4

William Collins' dream of knowledge for all began with the publication of his first book in 1819.
A self-educated mill worker, he not only enriched millions of lives, but also founded a flourishing publishing house. Today, staying true to this spirit, Collins books are packed with inspiration, innovation and practical expertise.
They place you at the centre of a world of possibility and give you exactly what you need to explore it.

Collins. Freedom to teach.

Published by Collins
An imprint of HarperCollins*Publishers*
The News Building
1 London Bridge Street
London
SE1 9GF

HarperCollins*Publishers*
Macken House, 39/40 Mayor Street Upper,
Dublin 1, D01 C9W8, Ireland

Browse the complete Collins catalogue at
www.collins.co.uk

© HarperCollins*Publishers* Limited 2021

10 9 8 7

ISBN 978-0-00-836919-4

British Library Cataloguing-in-Publication Data
A catalogue record for this publication is available from the British Library.

Author: Karen Morrison and Jennifer Martin
Series Editor: Daphne Paizee
Publisher: Elaine Higgleton
Product Manager: Lucy Cooper
Development Editor: Cait Hawkins
Project Manager: Lucy Hobbs
Proof reader: Michael Lamb
Cover design: Gordon MacGilp
Cover artwork: QBS Learning
Internal design: Ken Vail Graphic Design
Typesetter: QBS Learning
Illustrations: QBS Learning and Beehive Illustrations
Production controller: Lyndsey Rogers
Printed in India by Multivista Global Pvt. Ltd.

Text acknowledgements
The publishers gratefully acknowledge the permission granted to reproduce the copyright material in this book. Every effort has been made to trace copyright holders and to obtain their permission for the use of copyright material. The publishers will gladly receive any information enabling them to rectify any error or omission at the first opportunity.

HarperCollins*Publishers* Limited for extracts and artwork from: *Bugs!* by Sam McBratney, illustrated by Eric Smith, text © 2010 Sam McBratney. *Animal Ancestors* by Jon Hughes, text © 2006 Jon Hughes. *Peter and the Wolf* by Diane Redmond, illustrated by John Bendall-Brunello, text © 2007 Diane Redmond. *The Pied Piper of Hamelin* by Jane Ray, illustrated by Jane Ray, text © 2011 Jane Ray. *Chicken Licken* by Jeremy Strong, illustrated by Tony Blundell, text © 2007 Jeremy Strong. *The Ultimate World Quiz* by Claire Llewellyn, text © 2008 Claire Llewellyn. *The Olympic Games* by John Foster, text © 2009 John Foster. *Your Senses* by Sally Morgan, illustrated by Maurizio De Angelis, text © 2012 Sally Morgan.

Photo acknowledgements
The publishers wish to thank the following for permission to reproduce photographs. Every effort has been made to trace copyright holders and to obtain their permission for the use of copyright materials. The publishers will gladly receive any information enabling them to rectify any error or omission at the first opportunity.

p24a Bird Hunter/Shutterstock, p24b Eric Isselee/Shutterstock, p24c Inna G/Shutterstock, p24d Tsnebula23/Shutterstock, p24e Lakov Filimonov/Shutterstock, p24f Narupon Nimpaiboon/Shutterstock, p43 VAKSMAN VOLODYMYR/Shutterstock, p75 Rawpixel/Shutterstock, p99 Ververidis Vasilis/Shutterstock, p102 Vasyl Shulga/Shutterstock, p135l arogant/Shutterstock, p135r ArtMari/Shutterstock, p141a Svetlana Foote/Shutterstock, p141b Rebius/Shutterstock, p141c nwdph/Shutterstock, p143 Eric Isselee/Shutterstock

With thanks to the following teachers and schools for reviewing materials in development: Hawar International School; Melissa Brobst, International School of Budapest; Niki Tzorzis, Pascal Primary School Lemessos.

Contents

Unit 1 Fun and games

Week 1 Hobbies and sports

1 **Rearrange each set of words to make a sentence about sports and hobbies. Remember to punctuate your sentences correctly.**

a) likes surf to brother my

_____

b) prefer play to we badminton

_____

c) we playing hate table tennis

_____

d) on watching TV I enjoy basketball

_____

2 **Write two of your own sentences about what you like to do in your free time.**

_____

_____

_____

3 **Answer 'Yes I do' or 'No I don't'.**

a) Do you love to swim? _____

b) Do you like surfing? _____

c) Do you enjoy shooting hoops? _____

d) Do you prefer playing football to baseball? _____

e) Do you hate to play tennis? _____

4 **Complete the sentences.**

I like to _____.

I don't like to _____.

5 **Look at the pictures in question 6. Write the name of the sport above each picture. Choose from the box.**

badminton	basketball	cricket	cycling	football
surfing	swimming	table tennis	tennis	

6 **Unscramble the letters next to each picture. Write the correct name of a piece of clothing or equipment used in the sport.**

a)

cricket

_____

teckswi

_____

b)

_____

wimmisng ostcmue

_____

c)

_____

rekcat

_____

d)

_____

fursroabd

_____

e)

_____

ttushelccok

_____

f)

_____

poho

_____

g)

_____

labl

_____

h)

_____

ccleiby

_____

i)

_____

blate

_____

7 **What do you like to do in your free time? Complete the table about your favourite activity.**

Write the name of your favourite activity.	When do you do this activity?	Where do you do this activity?
_____ _____	_____ _____	_____ _____
When did you start this activity?	What equipment do you need?	What is your favourite part of this activity?
_____ _____ _____ _____	_____ _____ _____ _____	_____ _____ _____ _____

8 **Choose a word from the box to complete the sentences.**

a) I like to _____ cricket.

b) Sara prefers to _____ ballet.

c) Amira enjoys _____ music on her guitar.

d) Jo likes _____ fishing with his uncle.

e) Mai loves to _____ handstands against the wall.

f) We really enjoy _____ computer games.

do	doing
go	going
play	playing

g) Lin and her family are _____ to watch the match.

h) They are _____ judo in the hall next door.

i) My neighbours want to _____ surfing tomorrow.

9 **Decide where you can hide a geocache in your school. Draw a map to show where it is.**

10 **Write some instructions for your class to find your geocache. Use as many of the words in the box as you can.**

across	along	down	out of	into
through	to	towards	up	

11 **Look at each picture. Choose the best word from the box to complete the sentence.**

bounce	catch	dive	kick
ride	score	stop	throw

a)

The boy has to _____ the ball.

b)

The cyclist wants to _____ her bike.

c)

The goalie has to _____ the ball.

d)

My friend wants to _____ into the pool.

e)

The girls have to _____ the ball to each other.

f)

Her brother wants to _____ a fish.

g)

The basketball player has to _____ the ball before he throws it.

h)

The player wants to _____ a goal for his team.

8

Week 2 Outdoor adventures

1 **Read the nouns. Find each item in the picture. Draw a line to match each item to its name.**

| tree | mountain | bear | hiker | sky | path |

| rock | bag | lunch | Thermos | map | grass |

2 **Circle the correct word in each sentence.**

a) The (hiker / hikers) is hungry.

b) The hiker is sitting next to a (mountain / path).

c) He is wearing (shoe / shoes).

d) When the hiker is thirsty he drinks (water / waters).

3 **Complete these sentences using the picture and words from activity 1.**

a) There are many _____, _____ and _____ in a nature reserve.

b) The hiker packed _____, _____ and _____ in his bag.

4 **Look at the picture carefully. Tell your partner what you can see.**

5 **Look at the picture and correct the sentences.**

a) The bear is eating. _____

b) The hiker can see the bear. _____

c) The bear looks very dangerous. _____

d) The hiker is looking at his map. _____

e) The hiker is sitting on the ground. _____

6 **Read the sentences. Colour the picture to match.**

The grass is green and the sky is blue.

The tree trunks are brown and so is the bear.

The hiker is wearing red boots and a yellow shirt.

The backpack is green.

7 Write a number to answer each question.

   a) How many bears can you see? _____

   b) How many mountains can you see? _____

   c) How many backpacks can you see? _____

   d) How many rocks can you see? _____

8 Choose an adjective to describe each noun. You can choose from the box or you can use your own. Read your sentences aloud.

delicious	exciting	funny	long	loud
massive	nice	scary	small	strange

   a) This is a _____ poem about going hiking.

   b) I thought this was a _____ poem.

   c) The hiker packed a _____ lunch.

   d) As he walked he heard _____ noises.

   e) He tripped over a _____ rock.

   f) He walked under a _____ waterfall.

   g) When the hiker turned around he saw a _____ bear.

9 Underline the names of the things you can eat. Circle the names of the two things you would most like to eat.

cake	sweets	cheese	rocks	trees
juice	apples	fruit	socks	vegetables
bread	chocolate	ice cream		

10 **Draw pictures of pizza toppings in the boxes. Write a sentence about each picture. Use the examples to help.**

I like some delicious cheese on my pizza.	I want four red tomatoes on my pizza.

11 Read the list of items that Juan packed for a hiking trip.

rope	matches
plastic bags	spare socks
sharp knife	warm jacket
compass	torch
watch	water
first aid kit	

a) Underline the uncountable nouns.

b) Choose three items. Say why each one is important to have if you go hiking.

Item 1: _____

Item 2: _____

Item 3: _____

12 Pedro made a list of silly things to take on a hike as a joke. Read his list.

1. a glass rope _____

2. a paper water bottle _____

3. a stone torch _____

4. a wooden backpack _____

5. a metal rubbish bag _____

6. plastic matches _____

7. a rubber knife _____

8. a cement jacket _____

a) Cross out the adjectives.

b) Rewrite the list with a more suitable adjective to describe each item.

13 Complete these sentences with prepositions.

a) The hiker walked _____ the tree.

b) He took a sandwich _____ his backpack.

c) He walked _____ the trees _____ the waterfall.

d) He hiked _____ to the top of the hill.

e) After the hike, he walked away _____ the park.

14 Complete this email about a hike to send to a friend. Look back at the poem in the Student's Resource Book for ideas to help.

Dear _____,

Yesterday, I went on a hike.

I woke up early and _____

_____

I walked _____

_____

The weather was _____

_____

At the end of the hike I _____

_____

Best wishes,

_____

Week 3 **Playing around**

1 **Read about the two games on page 8 of the Student's Resource Book. Complete the table to compare them.**

	Gonggi nori	Keeper of the Fire
Where does this game come from?		
What do you need to play it?		
What do you have to do?		
Who is the winner?		

2 **Write the instruction words.**

a) _____ the stones onto the ground.

b) _____ up one and _____ it into the air.

c) _____ up another stone.

d) _____ the stone you tossed in the air.

e) _____ one person to be the fire keeper.

f) _____ in the middle next to the sticks.

g) _____ your hands in your lap.

3 **Choose words from the box to complete the sentences. You can use some words more than once.**

a few   all   a lot of   both   many   some

a) Should I pick up _____ or _____ of the stones?

b) If you throw two stones you must try to catch _____ of them.

c) You only need to grab _____ of the sticks.

d) _____ people can play at the same time.

e) You can play with _____ stones or just _____.

f) There are _____ sticks in the pile.

g) The game of jacks is played in _____ different countries.

h) _____ of my friends are really good at games.

4 **Write 'a' or 'the' to complete the sentences about traditional games.**

a) First you pick up _____ stones.

b) You toss the stones into _____ air.

c) You try to catch all _____ stones.

d) One person is _____ fire keeper.

e) They have _____ pile of sticks.

f) The fire keeper wears _____ blindfold.

5 **Find out about another traditional game. Complete this information sheet about the game.**

Where does this game come from?	
What do you need to play it?	
How do you play it?	
How many people can play?	
Who is the winner?	

6 **Read the statements. Draw lines to match those that have the same meaning.**

It was a draw. ●   ● It was a home game.

I lost. ●   ● I won.

Whose turn is it? ●   ● Both teams got the same score.

We played at our school. ●   ● I didn't win.

Our team is top of the league. ●   ● Take turns.

I came first. ●   ● Who is next?

Go one after the other. ●   ● Our team is the best of our group.

7 **Zara is chatting to her friend Mariam online. Complete the last chat box.**

> **Zara:** We played a fun word game at school today. We had to make words all starting with the same letter.

> **Mariam:** Oh that sounds hard. How do you play it?

> **Zara:** Someone chooses a letter. Like M. Then you …
>
> _____
>
> _____
>
> _____
>
> _____.

8 **Write each set of words in alphabetical order.**

a) big   blue   beautiful   bright   balloons

_____   _____   _____   _____   _____

b) rosy   red   ripe   raspberries

_____   _____   _____   _____

c) gentle   green   grumpy   giant

_____   _____   _____   _____

d) clumsy   crazy   colourful   caterpillar

_____   _____   _____   _____

e) frilly   floppy   flat   fabulous   frogs

_____   _____   _____   _____

Unit 2 Is it true?

Week 1 In the rainforest

1 **Can you name these animals? Unscramble the letters.**

a) rptai   **b)** hepelnta   **c)** grauja   **d)** tba

_____ _____ _____ _____

e) pspsherorga   **f)** ymnoek   **g)** dipsre   **h)** keasn

_____ _____ _____ _____

2 **Complete the sentences comparing the animals. A clue is given after each sentence.**

a) An elephant is _____ than a jaguar. (big)

b) A spider is _____ than a monkey. (small)

c) A snake is _____ than a grasshopper's leg. (long)

d) A bat flies _____ than a bird. (fast)

e) A jaguar is _____ than a tapir. (beautiful)

3 **Choose any two of the animals. Write a sentence describing each animal.**

1: _____

_____

2: _____

_____

4 **Some visitors are meeting their guide for a tour of the rainforest. What does he tell them?**

Write three things that the guide plans to do. Complete sentences a) to c) with 'going to'.

a) We are going to _____ _____

b) _____ _____

c) _____ _____

Write three things that the guide predicts they will do. Complete sentences d) to f) with 'will'.

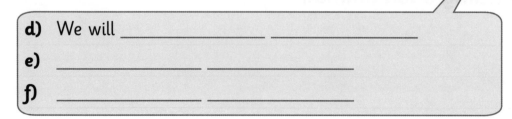

d) We will _____ _____

e) _____ _____

f) _____ _____

5 **What would the tour guide say about his day? Fill the gaps. Use the past simple form of the verbs at the end of the sentences.**

a) Today I _took_ some tourists to walk through the rainforest. (take)

b) They _____ very excited about the tour. (are)

c) We _____ carefully behind each other. (walk)

d) We _____ a tarantula spider. (see)

e) One man _____ such a big fright! (get)

f) The spider _____ onto his shoulder. (crawl)

g) He _____ it was a leaf falling from a tree. (think)

h) I _____ he would scream! (know)

i) He _____ all the way back to the bus! (run)

j) It _____ very funny! (is)

6 **Complete these sentences with two things each animal can do.**

a) A bat can _____.

b) A snake can _____.

c) A frog can _____.

7 **Read the names of the rainforest animals. Write them in order from the smallest to the biggest animal.**

| bat   elephant   frog   moth   snake   tapir |

_____   _____   _____

_____   _____   _____

8 Write a short report about a tour that someone took in a rainforest yesterday. Write four sentences, using the verbs below.

knew   thought   took   was

_____

_____

_____

_____

9 Look at the pictures. Read the sentences about each picture. Make up a different ending for the sentence for each picture.

a) This is the man who touched a spider.

This is the man _____

_____.

b) That is the woman who shouted at him to leave the spider alone.

That is the woman _____

_____.

c) Here is the photo that I took of the tarantula spider.

Here is the photo _____

_____.

d) There is the torch that I dropped.

There is the torch _____

_____.

e) This is where we saw the tarantula spider.

This is _____

_____.

10 Read the clues. Complete the crossword puzzle.

Down

1 These are creatures that do not have legs. Some of them are very poisonous.

2 This is a very large spider. It is very hairy.

3 We say that the trees form a _____ in the forest.

4 This mammal is related to the elephant, but is much smaller. It can be found in a rainforest.

5 These creatures live in caves and fly at night.

6 Tree frogs like to eat this type of insect.

Across

7 These get eaten by frogs.

8 Snakes like to eat these creatures.

9 This is place that gets a lot of rain throughout the year.

10 A rainforest is filled with these. They get cut down by humans.

11 **Draw a line from the animal to words that describe how the animal moves. Use a dictionary to find the meanings of any words you don't know.**

slide   a)   fly

sneak   soar

b)

creep   dive

c)

leap   climb

crawl   d)   walk

prowl   run

e)

clamber   stalk

f)

swing   jump

12 **Write your own sentences to describe how each of these animals move. Use the example to help you.**

Example: The monkey _clambers and swings in the trees._

The jaguar _____.

The snake _____.

The bat _____.

24

Week 2 Bugs are helpful

1   Read the poem *Bugs Are Helpful* on pages 12–13 of the Student's Resource Book again with your partner. Look at the things that bugs do and decide if they are good or bad. Write them in the correct column.

> make us sick   make food go bad   make some kinds of rubbish disappear
> make things smell bad   make food for plants

Good things	Bad things

Do you think bugs are good or bad? Why?

I think bugs are _____ because _____

_____

_____.

2   Which senses do you use? Write the missing words. Use the words in the box to help you.

> taste   hear   touch   see   smell

a) I _____ the bin with my fingers.

b) I _____ the rotten food with my nose.

c) I _____ the cans fall into the bin with my ears.

d) I _____ the food with my tongue.

e) I _____ the rubbish with my eyes.

3 **Circle the best word to describe the rubbish in each sentence.**

   a) The fish smells (bad / fresh).

   b) The meat smells (fresh / rotten).

   c) The bottles are (empty / full).

   d) The boxes are (strong / broken).

   e) The paper is (torn / clean).

4 **What do bugs do? Draw lines to match the beginning of the sentence to suitable endings.**

We are bugs and we …

make things rot.

make things smell nice.

make food taste good.

make things smell bad.

make last year's leaves rot.

cause decay.

make people sick.

5 **You have put the rubbish in the bin in the picture on page 26. Answer the questions to say what you are going to do next.**

Example: Are you going to cook the meat?

No, I'm not going to cook the meat!

a) Are you going to eat the fish?

_____

b) Are you going to take the rubbish outside?

_____

c) Are you going to wash your hands carefully?

_____

6 **Where can you find bugs? What can they do? Make a list.**

_____

_____

7 **Write some questions you can ask someone about a visit to a doctor. Use the example and the words to help you.**

Example: _When did you visit the doctor?_

a) Why did _____ ?

b) How _____ feel?

c) What _____ have to do?

d) _____ have to take some medicine?

e) _____ the medicine taste like?

f) _____ feel better?

8 **Kira has cut her foot. Read this conversation between Kira and the nurse at the clinic aloud with a partner.**

Nurse: What is the matter?

Kira: I cut my foot on broken glass.

Nurse: Let me have a look.

Kira: There is a lot of blood.

Nurse: Yes. That is because the cut is deep. You have to have a few stitches.

Kira: Will it hurt a lot?

Nurse: No, it won't hurt much.

Draw Kira's accident.

9 **Imagine you are Kira. Complete these sentences to tell someone else what happened.**

a) I cut _____

_____.

b) I had to go to the _____

_____.

c) I had to have _____

_____.

d) It didn't _____

_____.

10 **What do you have to do if you cut yourself? Why?**

You have to _____ because

_____

_____.

11 **Cross out the wrong word(s) in each sentence.**

a) My leg is bleeding (many / a lot).

b) I have (some / one) plasters.

c) You will not need (many / much) stitches.

d) I do not have (few / much) money.

e) It will not cost too (lots / much).

f) I think you need (a few /a lot) stitches.

12 Complete these sentences about yourself.

I always _____.

I sometimes _____.

I never _____.

I often _____.

I always _____ before school.

I sometimes _____ before school.

I never _____ in cold water.

I often _____ my clothes.

I often _____ the garbage.

I never _____ my family.

I always _____ on a Monday.

I sometimes _____ in the afternoon.

13 Write your own sentences.

I always _____.

I often _____.

I sometimes _____.

I never _____.

Week 3 Animals from another time

1 **Read the information about animals from another time on pages 14–15 of the Student's Resource Book. Tick the boxes that apply to each animal.**

	Meat-eater	Plant-eater	Larger than living relative	Larger than a person
The giant short-faced kangaroo				
The mammoth				
The Indrik Beast				
The Terror bird				
The Argentine bird				

2 **Answer the following questions.**

a) The mammoth lived underground, didn't it?

_____

b) The Argentine bird ate small lizards, mice and rabbits, didn't it?

_____

c) The Indrik Beast was the smallest mammal to ever live on land, wasn't it? _____

d) Elephants are the closest living relatives of mammoths, aren't they?

_____

e) The giant short-faced kangaroo hunted fish, didn't it?

_____

f) Another name for a Terror bird is *Titanis*, isn't it?

_____

3 **Label the pictures with the names of an animal from the box.**

Argentine bird   Indrik Beast   mammoth   *Procoptodon*   *Titanis*

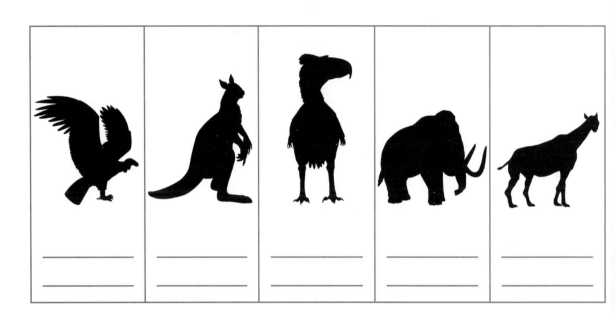

| _____ | _____ | _____ | _____ | _____ |

4 **Choose the correct word to complete each sentence. Write the word on the line.**

a) The Argentine bird was the _____ ever flying bird. (smallest/largest/heaviest)

b) The Argentine bird ate _____ animals such as lizards and mice. (small/smaller/smallest)

c) The Indrik Beast was much _____ than the largest rhino. (heavy/heavier/heaviest)

d) The Indrik Beast was the _____ ever mammal to walk on land. (large/larger/largest)

e) The mammoth's _____ living relative is the elephant. (close/closer/closest)

f) The giant short-faced kangaroo was much _____ than a modern kangaroo. (big/bigger/biggest)

5 **Draw a picture of an imaginary animal that could have lived in your country thousands of years ago.**

6 **Write information about your animal. Complete the table.**

What is the animal's name?	What does the animal eat?
_____	_____
Where does the animal live?	How does the animal move?
_____	_____
Describe the animal.	
_____	
_____	

7 **Two learners are talking about their class project on animals from another time. Choose words from the box to complete the sentences correctly.**

could   may   might

Tracey: How should we present our information?

Franz: We _____ make a poster.

Tracey: Yes, we _____.

Franz: We _____ draw the outline of a mammoth and write our information inside it.

Tracey: I think that _____ be too difficult to do.

Franz: No, it will not be too difficult. Let me show you. _____ I borrow your pencil?

Tracey: Yes, you _____.

Franz: If we work hard, we _____ have the best poster in the class!

8 **Circle the correct words to make the sentences true.**

a) The mammoth is (alive / extinct) today.

b) The mammoth was a type of (elephant / rhino).

9 **Say whether each statement is true or false.**

a) The Terror bird could fly. _____

b) The *Procoptodon* lived in Australia. _____

10 Write the missing words.

a) The *Argentavis* ate animals such as _____,
    _____ and _____.

b) The *Argentavis* was the _____ ever flying bird.

c) The Indrik Beast was the largest ever animal to _____
    on land.

11 Answer these questions in full sentences.

a) What does 'extinct' mean?

    _____

b) Where did the Argentine bird live?

    _____

c) What did mammoths eat?

    _____

d) Why could the Terror bird not fly?

    _____

12 Words from pages 14–15 of the Student's Resource Book are given in the first column. Circle the word in the second column that is closest in meaning to each one.

1 huge	small	massive	invisible
2 attackers	friends	enemies	intruders
3 hunted	chased	searched	followed
4 hind	front	middle	back
5 strong	heavy	powerful	cheeky

Unit 3 Fire!

Week 1 The Great Fire of London

1 **Skim read the infographic about the Great Fire of London on Student's Resource Book pages 16–17 to find the answers to these questions.**

   a) When did the fire start?
   b) How long did the fire burn for?
   c) Where did the fire start?
   d) How many people died in the fire?
   e) Were there any fire engines?

2 **There are fifteen adjectives that describe fire in the word puzzle. Find them and write them below the puzzle. The first letter(s) of each word is given.**

b	y	i	s	b	u	r	n	i	n	g	k	i	e
g	h	s	m	y	e	e	k	e	t	d	r	e	d
u	n	c	o	n	t	r	o	l	l	a	b	l	e
b	i	a	k	d	t	i	e	t	l	n	o	t	s
r	r	r	y	e	l	l	o	w	o	g	e	e	t
i	c	y	s	a	i	d	r	c	t	e	u	i	r
g	e	m	e	d	s	h	a	g	s	r	i	t	u
h	i	w	i	l	d	r	n	u	h	o	t	v	c
t	r	s	b	y	s	f	g	m	h	u	i	d	t
g	e	h	r	e	c	n	e	t	i	s	t	r	i
r	b	l	a	z	i	n	g	f	t	u	e	c	v
f	i	e	r	c	e	r	f	r	e	e	u	v	e

bl_____   bu_____   sc_____   br_____   w_____

r_____   y_____   o_____   sm_____   fi_____

h_____   de_____   de_____   da_____   un_____

3 **Write the comparative and superlative forms of the adjectives in the table.**

hot	hotter	hottest
wild		
bright		
smoky		
scary		
dangerous		
destructive		
deadly		

4 **Circle the best word to describe the nouns in the following sentences.**

a) The fire was very (hotter / hot).

b) Everyone was (frightened / more frightened).

c) My family buried their (most precious / more precious) things to protect them.

d) My neighbour was very (helpful / more helpful).

e) The smoke in that building is the (thicker / thickest) – no one can see anything!

f) The wind made the fire (more destructive / most destructive).

5 **Circle the correct adjective in each sentence.**

a) The fire was very (dark / bright).

b) The girl was (happy / sad) that her house burned down.

c) The people filled (wooden / broken) buckets with water.

d) The (raging / gentle) fire burned the houses down.

e) The (wooden / brick) houses burned down easily.

6 **Look at each picture. Write down four adjectives to describe each one.**

a)

The children are …

_____scared_____

_____

_____

_____

b)

The house is …

_____

_____

_____

_____

c)

The flames are …

_____

_____

_____

_____

d)

The smoke is …

_____

_____

_____

_____

7 **Choose a word from the box to complete each sentence.**

any   anything   nothing   some   something

a) We need water. Do you have _____?

b) The smoke is so thick, I can't see _____ .

c) I think I see _____ .

d) The fire is too strong. _____ can stop it.

e) We have to think of _____ .

f) Is there _____ we can do to help put out the flames?

8 **Imagine you were one of the people in the picture. Write words to describe what you could see, hear, smell and feel during the fire.**

See:	Hear:
Smell:	Feel:

9 **Read the diary extracts written by Samuel Pepys on PCM 10 again. Look at the pictures and write 'this', 'that', 'these' or 'those' to complete the sentences.**

a) Where do you want me to put _____?

b) We will need to pack _____ as well.

c) Please put _____ in a box.

d) You can leave _____ on the table.

10 **Draw lines from the beginning of each sentence to a suitable ending.**

a) There were many •   • in the city.

b) People were worried
about catching •   • buildings.

c) The buildings were made •   • the plague.

d) Some buildings were •   • from wood.

e) The streets were •   • four storeys high.

f) Fires often started •   • very narrow.

11 **Write a conversation between a reporter and Samuel Pepys. Complete the sentences. Read your conversation aloud with a partner.**

Reporter: Good day, Sir. I believe you are the man who buried important papers in his garden.

Samuel Pepys: _____.

Reporter: What time did you wake up?

Samuel Pepys: _____.

Reporter: Who woke you up?

Samuel Pepys: _____.

Reporter: What did you do next?

Samuel Pepys: _____.

Reporter: Where did you go?

Samuel Pepys: _____.

Reporter: Then what did you do?

Samuel Pepys: _____.

Week 2 Firefighters

1 **Read the text on Student's Resource Book page 18 again. Find the correct ending for each sentence from the box. Copy the ending next to the beginning of the sentence.**

… to reach fires on small boats.	… to pour water on fires.
… in teams to put out fires.	… to reach fires at the top of buildings.

a) Firefighters work _____.

b) Firefighters use jet skis _____.

c) Firefighters use ladders _____.

d) Firefighters use hosepipes _____.

2 **Unscramble the words to make sensible sentences.**

a) out on put land. fires Firefighters

_____

b) water-bomb Helicopters forest fires.

_____

c) oil fire saw well this from Astronauts space.

_____

d) shallow Jet in skis water. work

_____

e) foam The stops spreading. smoke

_____

3 **Imagine you are a firefighter and that you had to put out a fire on a ship at sea. Write a short description of what you did. Start like this:**

Yesterday we got a call from a ship's captain. She reported a fire on a fishing boat in the bay. Some fishermen were

4 **Unscramble the letters and write the words.**

a) refi negein _____

b) brnu _____

c) lsfame _____

d) spiespohe _____

e) sifer _____

5 **Look at the picture and read the two sentences.**

Sentence A: The firefighter is holding
the hosepipe.

Sentence B: The tired firefighter is
struggling to hold the
heavy hosepipe.

a) Which sentence is more interesting?

_____

b) Why is it more interesting?

_____

6 **Read these sentences. How could you make them
more interesting? Write your interesting sentences.**

a) The tree is burning.

_____

b) The wind is blowing.

_____

c) The man is shouting.

_____

7 **Now write three interesting sentences of your own
about the picture.**

1: _____

2: _____

3: _____

8 **Imagine you are a firefighter captain. Your job is to train new firefighters to put out fires and use the equipment properly. Complete the sentences.**

a) When you hear the siren, you have to _____

_____.

b) After you hear the siren, you have to _____

_____.

c) Before you climb up a ladder, you have to _____

_____.

d) When you can't open a door, you have to _____

_____.

e) When you can't breathe easily, you have to _____

_____.

9 **Write down three sentences giving advice to firefighters. Use the information below. An example has been done for you.**

You have to wear a mask because the smoke is dangerous.

_____

_____

_____

_____

_____

Firefighters need special tools and safety equipment. Why would they need the following items?

an axe, a helmet, a mask, gloves, heavy coats, rubber boots

10 **Answer these questions in complete sentences.**

a) Why must you not hide away inside a house if it is on fire?

_____

b) What did people do to try and put out the Great Fire of London?

_____

c) What do firefighters use to put out fires on small boats?

_____

d) What dangers do firefighters face?

_____

e) What do firefighters use to put out chemical fires?

_____

11 **Read the words that tell us more about a firefighter. Use a dictionary to help you if you do not know what the words mean. Write two interesting sentences to describe a firefighter.**

brave	hungry
courageous	strong
determined	tired
experienced	young
friendly	

1: _____

_____

2: _____

_____

12 **Work in pairs. Complete the table of words. Use a dictionary to help you.**

Words with 'fire'	Meaning	Word in my first language
fire station fire brigade fireplace firework		

Can you add more words with 'fire'?

13 **Complete these sentences to show what you learned about fires and firefighting in this week.**

a) Call the fire station if _____.

b) Water cannot be used to put out a chemical fire, so

_____.

c) Firefighters have to wear special suits when _____.

d) When firefighters can't get into a house, they have to

_____.

e) You must know where _____.

f) You must never hide _____.

g) There is a lot of cleaning up to do after _____.

h) Firefighters will always help when _____.

14 Choose the correct answer. Circle the letter.

1 What don't we use fire for?

a) To give us heat.

b) To give us light.

c) To make forests grow.

2 What don't we use to put out fires?

a) Air

b) Water

c) Foam

3 Which of the following statements is true?

a) You can play with matches.

b) You can only play with matches when your parents are home.

c) You must NEVER play with matches.

4 Which of the following statements is true?

a) It is easier to breathe in a fire when you stay low.

b) It is easier to breathe in a fire when you stay healthy.

c) It is easier to breathe in a fire when you stay under the bed.

5 Which of the following statements is true?

a) When you run, the flames burn slower.

b) When you run, you put out the flames.

c) When you run, the flames burn faster.

15 Answer 'true' or 'false'.

a) People used buckets of water to put out the fire in London in 1666.
_____

b) Water puts out chemical fires. _____

c) Helicopters can be used to put out forest fires. _____

d) Jet skis can be used to put out fires on oil tankers. _____

Week 3 Puff, the Dragonsaurus

1 **Listen to the story about Puff. Number the pictures in order to show what happened.**

2 **Circle the correct words to answer each question.**

a) Who is shouting at Puff's family?

The (monster / tree) is shouting at Puff's family.

b) Where does Puff's family live?

Puff's family live (in / on) a cave.

c) What does Puff want to do?

Puff wants to (read a book / help) his family.

3 **Answer these questions in complete sentences.**

a) Who did Puff talk to first outside the cave?

_____

_____

b) Who else did Puff talk to?

_____

_____

c) What did Puff eat?

_____

_____

4 **Write two sentences describing what happened after Puff ate the red berry.**

1: _____

_____

2: _____

_____

5 **Complete these sentences. Try to make them as interesting as you can. Use the example to help you.**

Example: The tree laughs *unkindly at Puff*.

a) The rock speaks _____.

b) Puff runs _____.

c) The monster shouts _____.

6 **Write three of your own sentences about the story.**

1: _____

_____

2: _____

_____

3: _____

_____

7 **Complete the sentences with a verb from box 1 and an adverb from box 2.**

1
| lived   ran   read   ~~snored~~   spoke   licked   walked |

2
| carefully   happily   ~~loudly~~   quickly   quietly   rudely   sadly |

Example: The monster *snored* *loudly*.

a) Puff didn't want to _____ _____.

b) He _____ _____ away from the cave.

c) The tree and the rock both _____ _____ to Puff.

d) Puff _____ _____ away.

e) He found a red berry and _____ it _____.

f) The dragonsaurus family _____ _____ ever after.

8 **Choose words from the box to complete these sentences.**

> fire   fur   glass   ice

a) The wind felt cold, like _____.

b) The rock felt hot, like _____.

c) The grass felt soft, like _____.

d) The stone felt smooth, like _____.

9 **Describe the monster that wanted to chase the dinosaurs away from their cave. Then draw it.**

a) The monster looked like _____.

b) He had eyes like _____.

c) His ears were like _____.

d) His teeth were like _____.

e) His voice was like _____.

f) He walked like _____.

g) The monster snored like _____.

10 **Choose words from the box to complete these sentences. You will use some of the words more than once.**

at	in	from	of	outside	with

a) Puff's family lived _____ a cave.

b) The story takes place _____ the autumn.

c) Puff's family ran away _____ butterflies.

d) They were also scared _____ mice.

e) They trembled _____ fear when they heard the wind.

f) A monster stood _____ the cave.

g) He shouted _____ Puff and his family.

11 **Complete the following sentences.**

a) Puff wanted to help his family, so _____

_____.

b) The tree told Puff to go away before all _____

_____.

c) The rock told Puff to go away before he _____

_____.

d) Puff ate a berry, then _____

_____.

e) Puff ran home after _____

_____.

f) Fire came out when _____

_____.

Unit 4 Animal stories

Week 1 Peter and the Wolf

1 Write the names of the characters below their pictures.
Draw lines to match the characters to what they said.

a)

_____ •

• Go away. You're making
me dizzy.

b)

_____ •

• I'm going into the forest to
catch the big, bad wolf.

c)

_____ •

• Peter! I told you not to
play in the meadow. It's a
dangerous place!

d)

_____ •

• What kind of bird are you
if you can't swim?

e)

_____ •

• What kind of bird are you
if you can't fly?

2 Underline the sentence that matches each picture.

a) In front of the cottage, lay a big, green meadow.

b) Peter ran into the meadow and met his friend, Bird.

a) Duck waddled into the water and started to splash about.

b) The wolf, in his hurry to eat her, swallowed her whole.

a) As soon as Peter and Grandfather had gone, a big, grey wolf came creeping out of the forest.

b) Suddenly, Grandfather ran into the meadow, waving his arms.

a) Peter put a rope around the wolf's neck.

b) Bird flew round and round the wolf's head.

3 Look at the pictures. Write a sentence about what happened in each picture.

a)

_____

_____

_____

b)

_____

_____

_____

4 **Read the list of characteristics in the box. Look up the meaning of any words you don't understand and add them to your personal dictionary. Write the words that apply to each character in the correct columns. Some words might not apply to any of them.**

angry	clever	confident	determined	frightened
gentle	greedy	hopeful	inventive	kind
patient	sad	silly	sly	sneaky
strict	strong	surprised	unkind	

Peter	Grandfather	Wolf

What are your five best characteristics? Write them down.

Do you think other people would agree? Ask some people what they think your best characteristics are, to see if they agree or not.

5 **Choose interesting adjectives to complete these sentences.**

a) Peter is wearing a _____ shirt.

b) He is wearing _____ trousers.

c) The bird is sitting in the _____ tree.

d) The _____ cat wants to climb the tree.

e) The _____ duck is swimming in the _____ pond.

f) The Sun is shining. It is a _____ day.

g) The _____ grass feels _____.

> An adjective is a word that tells you more about a noun. For example, a **grey** day, a **stormy** sky, an **impatient** person.

6 **Answer these questions about the characters in *Peter and the Wolf*.**

a) Who was braver: Peter or his grandfather? _____

b) Which animal was the smallest? _____

c) Which animal was the cruelest? _____

d) Which character was the oldest? _____

7 **Complete each sentence with the correct word.**

a) Duck _____ (waddled / waddling) into the water and started to splash about.

b) You must _____ (fly / flying) round the wolf till he is sick and dizzy.

c) High up in the tree, Cat and Bird _____ (looking / looked) down at the wolf.

d) The wolf didn't _____ (see / saw) Peter.

e) The wolf _____ (feel / felt) the lasso when it was pulled tight around his tail.

f) Amazing! Let's _____ (take / taking) him to the zoo.

8 **Reread the story of *Peter and the Wolf*. Then underline the correct answer to the following questions.**

1 Why did Peter feel brave?

a) He could swim.

b) He was going to catch the big, bad wolf.

2 Where was Peter's favourite place to play?

a) The meadow

b) The zoo

3 How did Bird feel when he looked at Duck swimming in the water?

a) Cross that he could not swim too.

b) Happy that he could fly.

4 Why did Duck and Bird not see Cat creep up on them?

a) They were joking with each other.

b) They were arguing with each other.

5 How did Grandfather feel when he saw Peter in the meadow?

a) He felt very cross.

b) He felt sad.

6 How do you think Cat felt when he saw the wolf?

a) Scared

b) Excited

7 How do you think Peter felt when he saw the wolf eat Duck?

a) Happy

b) Cross

9 **Answer these questions about the story.**

a) Why does Peter want to go into the forest?

b) Does the wolf catch Cat?

c) Where do they take the wolf?

10 **Here are some sentences about the story of _Peter and the Wolf_. Use the words in the box to join some of the sentences.**

– Peter played with the animals.

– Grandfather said the meadow was dangerous.

– Wolf came from the forest.

– Wolf caught Duck.

– Peter, Bird and Cat made a plan.

– They caught Wolf.

after   before   then   when

Example: _Wolf caught Duck when he came from the forest._

1: _____

2: _____

3: _____

4: _____

11 **Each character has decided to do something. Write down what they say. Use the example to help you.**

Example: Peter has decided to go into the forest, so he says ...

      I'm _going to go to the forest_.

a) Cat has decided to catch Bird, so she says ...

    I'm _____

b) Duck has decided to swim in the water, so she says ...

    I'm _____

c) Peter has decided to put a rope around Wolf's neck, so he says ...

    I'm _____

12 **Someone is asking you what you think will happen in the story. Answer their questions. Use the example to help you.**

Example: What will Grandfather do?

Grandfather will fetch Peter.

a) What will Peter do?

_____

b) What will Duck do?

_____

c) What will Cat do?

_____

d) What will the wolf do?

_____

e) What will Bird do?

_____.

13 **Write your answers to these questions. Take turns to ask your partner each question. Read your answer when it is your turn.**

a) Have you ever heard the story about *Peter and the wolf*?

_____.

b) Have you ever seen a duck swim?

_____.

c) Have you ever heard a wolf howl?

_____.

d) Have you ever played a musical instrument?

_____.

e) Have you ever disobeyed someone?

_____.

f) Have you ever been to a zoo?

_____.

14 **Make up three questions of your own that start with 'Have you ever …?'. Read your questions to your partner and let them answer them.**

Question 1: Have you ever _____

_____?

Question 2: Have you ever _____

_____?

Question 3: Have you ever _____

_____?

15 **Read this information with your partner.**

> The **tale** of *Peter and the Wolf* was originally written as a musical by the Russian **composer** Sergei Prokofiev. The aim was to encourage children to enjoy classical **music**. In the musical version, each **character** is represented by a different musical **instrument**, and a **narrator** tells the story as the **orchestra** plays.

The meanings of the words in bold are given below. Write the correct word next to its definition.

a) _____ a person who tells a story

b) _____ a person who writes music

c) _____ another word for a story

d) _____ a person in a story or play

e) _____ you play this to make music

f) _____ the sound made by instruments playing together

g) _____ a group of musicians

Week 2 The Pied Piper of Hamelin

1 **Read the sentences about some rats. Draw a picture to show where the rat is in each one.**

The rat is in the rubbish bin.	The rat is on the floor.	The rat is at the end of the street.

2 **Choose prepositions of direction from the box to complete the sentences.**

> Prepositions can show direction. For example, The piper walked **towards** the river. The rats jumped **into** the water.

> from   into   out of   to   towards

a) Rats moved _____ Hamelin.

b) The people were scared to go _____ their homes.

c) A piper promised to move the rats _____ Hamelin.

d) The rats came _____ everywhere to follow the piper.

e) They followed the piper _____ the river.

f) The piper walked _____ the river.

g) The piper walked _____ the Mayor's office.

h) He took the children _____ a mountain.

3 **Make five sentences using the phrases in the circle. Start with the phrase in the middle. Choose a phrase from each ring. Write your sentences below the circle. Remember to punctuate them correctly.**

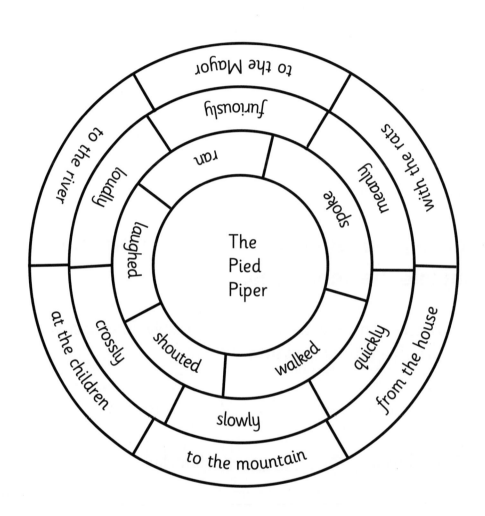

1: _____

2: _____

3: _____

4: _____

5: _____

4 **Draw a line to match the beginning of each sentence with a suitable ending.**

Once upon a time, on the banks of a river in Germany, ●	● a thousand gold coins.
	● into the river and so did the rats — every single one of them!
The little town grew very ●	● in the cupboards.
There were rats ●	● lay a small town called Hamelin.
In less than a week, ●	● on the outside of the door.
Just then, there was a loud knock ●	● rich and the people were very happy.
Pay me ●	● before the happy voices of other children were to be heard in the streets of Hamelin.
The Pied Piper walked ●	● the Pied Piper out of the town.
The Pied Piper shook his fist ●	● an army of rats had taken over the town.
The children followed ●	● at the Mayor.
Only one little boy remained ●	● and there stood a tall thin man dressed in brightly coloured clothes.
Many years were to pass ●	

There is an expression in English that says 'it is time to pay the piper'.

Find out what this expression means.

How could the saying apply to this story?

5   Think about the story. Discuss these questions in groups and then write your own answers.

a) Do you think the rats were dangerous?

_____

b) Do you think that the cats were scared of the rats?

_____

c) Do you think the Mayor was a good person?

_____

d) Where did the story happen?

_____

e) Where did the Pied Piper take the rats?

_____

f) Why was the Pied Piper angry with the Mayor?

_____

g) Do you think he was right to be angry?

_____

h) How did he punish the people of Hamelin?

_____

i) Do you think he was right to punish the citizens of Hamelin?

_____

j) Do you think the punishment was fair?

_____

k) What would you have done?

_____

6 **Read the news broadcast from Karen, the *Hamelin Daily News* reporter. Some of her words are missing. Can you write them into the gaps?**

> across   followed   happened   has told   have disappeared
> have never seen   into   led   out of   towards   walked

Studio: We are going over now to our reporter Karen, in Hamelin … Karen, tell us what happened today.

Reporter: Hello from the streets of Hamelin. I _____ terrible events like those here today. This morning, after the Pied Piper _____ the rats _____ the river and got rid of them, the Mayor wouldn't pay him the money he promised!

Studio: Oh dear – that's not very fair of him. What _____ next, Karen?

Reporter: Well, the Pied Piper wasn't happy, and began to play his flute again. Suddenly, all the children started to follow him _____ the town.

Studio: Oh no! Where are the children now, Karen?

Reporter: We don't know exactly. The Piper _____ _____ the bridge and_____ the mountain. The children _____ him and we don't know where they are. They _____.

Studio: Really? Oh dear. This is terrible news. How do you know about this?

Reporter: One little boy isn't with the other children because he can't walk very quickly. He _____ us all about it.

Studio: That's very sad news, Karen. We hope the citizens of Hamelin find their children very soon.

Act out the news report, in pairs.

7 **Read what the Pied Piper is thinking. Write the missing word in each thought. Choose words from the box. You can use words more than once.**

> already   always   ever   yet

I have
_____
got rid of all the rats.

They have
not paid me
_____.

Will they
_____
pay me?

They will never
_____
forget me!

I have
_____
got another plan!

You must
_____
keep a promise.

Week 3 Help! The Sky is Falling

1 **Read this version of the story. Use words from the box to complete the sentences. You may use each word more than once.**

after	before	so	then	when

Chicken Licken thought the sky was falling _____ an acorn fell onto his head. Chicken Licken did not stop to check what it was _____ he decided to tell the queen and king.

Henny Penny was curious, _____ she asked Chicken Licken what had happened. Cocky Locky joined Chicky and Henny Penny _____ he heard their story. _____, Turkey Lurkey also wanted to know where they were going.

Foxy Loxy was walking along _____ he saw Chicky and his friends. He asked them where they were going, _____ they told him. Foxy wanted to trick them _____ they went much further, _____ he told them to follow him. _____ a little while, Chicky and his friends arrived at Foxy Loxy's den where they were eaten for lunch!

2 **Complete the following sentences.**

a) Chicken Licken was scared, so _____

_____.

b) Turkey Lurkey was in the cabbage patch when _____

_____.

c) Henny Penny wanted to know what happened before

_____

_____.

d) Cocky Locky decided to go with them after _____

_____.

e) Foxy Loxy led them to his den and _____

_____.

3 Imagine you are trying to find out what happened to Chicken Licken and the other animals. Start with Chicken Licken. Draw arrows to show the order of the story.

Start

4 The trail seems to lead to Foxy Loxy's den. Make up three questions you would ask Foxy Loxy to find out more about what happened.

Question 1: _____

_____

Question 2: _____

_____

Question 3: _____

_____

5 **Here are some notes about the story _Chicken Licken_. Use the notes to write sentences to make a summary of the story. Don't forget to use connectives to join some of your sentences. Look at the example to help you.**

Notes:
– acorn fell on Chicken Licken's head
– Chicken Licken thought sky was falling
– Chicken Licken decided to ask queen what to do
– Chicken Licken told other birds
– other birds went with Chicken Licken to tell queen
– birds met Foxy Loxy
– Foxy Loxy said he knew the way to queen
– birds followed Foxy Loxy to his den.
– Foxy and family ate birds

Here are some useful connectives:

after	and	because	before	but	so	then	when

Example: _Chicken Licken thought the sky was falling after an acorn fell on his head._

_____

_____

_____

_____

_____

_____

6 **Complete the sentences about Chicken Licken and his friends.**

a) Instead of trying to tell the queen, Chicken Licken could

_____.

b) Instead of joining Chicken Licken, Henny Penny could

_____.

c) Instead of playing in the cabbage patch, Turkey Lurky could

_____.

d) Instead of tricking Chicken Licken and his friends, Foxy Loxy could

_____.

7 **Write 'might', 'may' or 'could' to complete this conversation.**

Chicken Licken: Foxy Loxy, _____ you tell us where we need to go?

Foxy Loxy: Yes, I _____ but you _____ still get lost.

Chicken Licken: But we need to speak to the queen. She is the only one who _____ save us!

Foxy Loxy: _____ I go with you?

Chicken Licken: Of course you may. Perhaps we _____ follow you.

Foxy Loxy: What a good idea! You _____ even get a surprise on the way. Ha ha ha!

8 **Write the animal name below each picture.**

a) This is a

_____.

b) This is a

_____.

c) This is a

_____.

d) This is a

_____.

e) This is a

_____.

f) This is a

_____.

g) This is a

_____.

h) This is a

_____.

i) This is a and a

_____ _____.

j) This is a

_____.

9 **Write into each speech bubble the noise the animal makes. Use the words in this list.**

bleats	clucks	crows	gobbles	honks	meows
moos	neighs	quacks	squeaks	tweets	

Unit 5 Our wonderful world

Week 1 More about our world

1 **Complete the information about yourself.**

My name:

My address:

My country:

The continent I live on:

2 **Complete the table with the missing adjectives and comparative and superlative forms.**

Adjective	Comparative	Superlative
large		
		slowest
	bigger	
		longest
tall		
dry		
	higher	
		closest
	farther (or: further)	
cool		

3 **Complete these comparisons. The words in brackets tell you what to compare.**

The continent I live on is _____ than Antarctica. (size)

The continent I live on is _____ than Antarctica. (temperature)

The continent I live on is closest to _____. (name of another continent)

The continent I live on is furthest away from _____. (name of another continent)

4 **The diagram shows each continent's share of all the land on Earth. Use the information on the diagram to list the names of the continents in order, from biggest to smallest.**

The size of the continents

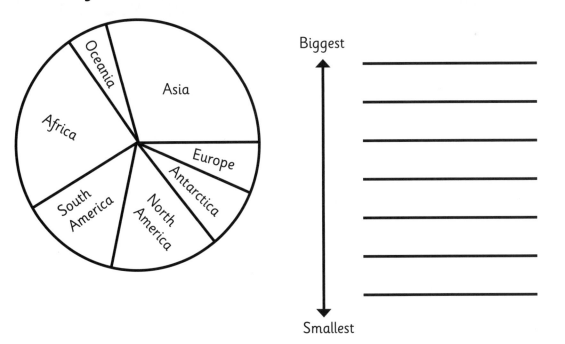

Biggest

Smallest

5 Tick 'true' or 'false'.

		true	false
a)	There are four continents.	☐	☐
b)	Asia is the biggest continent.	☐	☐
c)	Europe is the smallest continent.	☐	☐
d)	There are seven continents.	☐	☐
e)	South America is bigger than North America.	☐	☐
f)	Oceania is smaller than Africa.	☐	☐

6 An atlas is a book that contains maps and other information about places. What would you expect to find in each of these types of books?

a) an encyclopaedia: _____

b) a diary: _____

c) a dictionary: _____

d) a travel guide: _____

e) a textbook: _____

f) a manual: _____

g) a cookbook: _____

7 Choose the right words to fill the gaps.

a) There are _____ (much / many) countries, but only _____ (a few / a lot of) continents on Earth.

b) There are _____ (a lot of / every) rivers, but only _____ (much / a few) oceans.

c) _____ (Little / Many) people live in big cities, but only _____ (much / a few) people live in the desert.

d) There is not _____ (little / much) rain in the Atacama desert, but there is _____ (a lot of / many) rain in the Amazon rainforest.

e) There are _____ (each / a lot of) plants and animals in the Amazon rainforest, but not _____ (few / many) in the Atacama desert.

f) Very _____ (little / few) people live in Antarctica and they only spend _____ (a little / a few) time there.

g) There are rivers on _____ (every / many) continent, but not _____ (much / every) continent has cities.

h) _____ (A lot of / Each) continent has it's own special plants and animals.

i) People on _____ (a little / every) continent speak different languages. On most continents, people speak _____ (a lot / many) languages.

8 **Choose a continent and one country found on that continent. Work in groups to find the information you need to complete this fact file.**

Name of continent:	One country found on this continent:
What is the capital city of the country?	What is the currency of the country?
Interesting facts about the country:	Describe the country's flag:

9 **Read the sentences. Are they facts or opinions?**

a) Earth is a planet. _____

b) Earth is the best planet. _____

c) People do not live on Jupiter. _____

d) It would be fun to live on Jupiter. _____

10 **Imagine you are a scientist who is going to speak to a group of learners about Earth's continents and oceans. Write down three facts that you are going to tell the class.**

a) I am going to tell the class that _____.

b) I am going to tell the class that _____.

c) I am going to tell the class that _____.

11 **Write down two opinions you have about the continents and oceans.**

    a) I think that _____

    _____ .

    b) I think that _____

    _____ .

12 **Imagine you are going to listen to a scientist talk. What questions would you ask about the continents and oceans? Write three questions you could ask.**

    Question 1: _____

    Question 2: _____

    Question 3: _____

13 **Read each clue. Write the continent that matches it.**

    a) Only a few people live on this continent.

    _____

    b) This is the continent that is the largest one of all.

    _____

    c) This continent is where the 2016 Olympic Games were held.

    _____

    d) Australia and New Zealand form part of this continent.

    _____

    e) Lions, rhinos and elephants come from this continent.

    _____

    f) The first Olympic Games were held on this continent.

    _____

Week 2 Built wonders of the world

1   Write the name of each place under the picture. Look at pages 34–34 of the Student's Resource Book to check the spelling of each place name.

a)

_____

_____

b)

_____

_____

c)

_____

_____

d)

_____

_____

e)

_____

_____

f)

_____

_____

g)

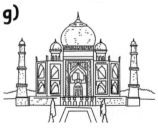

_____

_____

h)

_____

_____

2 **Read the two descriptions. Underline all the adjectives. Which places are being described? Write the names.**

a) This beautiful monument has a large domed roof in the centre with smaller towers around it. It is surrounded by lakes and peaceful gardens.	b) This ancient structure has a square base and the sides go up in large steps to a square top. There are steep ramps leading up to the top on all sides.
_____	_____

3 **Write a description of the Great Pyramid at Giza and the Colosseum in Rome. Use at least five adjectives.**

The Great Pyramid:	The Colosseum:

4 **Choose one of the places in the Student's Resource Book and complete the short Fact File.**

Name: _____

Where is it? _____

What is it? _____

An interesting fact: _____

5 Do a quick survey among learners in your class to find which three places most people want to visit. Ask at least five learners. Record the data in the tally table.

Place	Tally	Total
Great Pyramid		
Chichen Itza		
Petra		
Colosseum		
Machu Picchu		
Taj Mahal		
Burj Khalifa		
Great Wall of China		

6 Answer these questions about your survey.

a) Which place was most popular? _____

b) Which places were the second and third most popular places?

_____

c) Which place was chosen by the fewest learners? _____

d) Were there any places that were not chosen at all? _____

7 Write two sentences summarising what your survey tells you.

1: _____

2: _____

8 **Choose words from each column to make five different sentences. Write your sentences below the table.**

I	have	to see	the Colosseum	tomorrow.
They	planned	to visit	the city in the clouds	next week.
We	have decided	to explore	Burj Khalifa	in the afternoon.
			Petra	later.
	have agreed		the Great Wall of China	
			the Mayan pyramid	

1: _____

2: _____

3: _____

4: _____

5: _____

9 **Imagine you are going on a tour to see all of these places. Answer these questions about the trip you have planned.**

a) When are you going to visit the Colosseum?

_____

b) When are you going to explore the city in the clouds?

_____

c) Which place are you going to visit first?

_____

d) Which place are you going to explore last?

_____

10 Rewrite these sentences in the past tense.

Example: Tomorrow I will see the Statue of Liberty in New York.

Yesterday, *I saw the Statue of Liberty in New York.*

a) Next week we will walk around the pyramids.

Last week, _____.

b) Next year they will visit the Colosseum.

Last year, _____.

c) Next month I will see the Taj Mahal.

Last month, _____.

d) Tomorrow I am going to the pyramids.

Yesterday, _____.

11 Change the words in brackets to fit the sentences.

a) The Great Wall of China is the _____ (long) man-made structure in the world.

b) The pyramid of Chichen Itza is believed to be the _____ (great) of all Mayan temples.

c) Burj Khalifa is the _____ (tall) building in the world.

d) In my opinion, the Taj Mahal is the _____ (beautiful) building in India.

e) Most people think that the Sydney Opera House is the _____ (famous) building in Australia.

f) Stonehenge, in England, is much _____ (old) than the pyramids in Egypt

g) Machu Picchu is a _____ (cloudy) city than Barcelona.

h) My sister thinks that Shanghai is a much _____ (interesting) city than Singapore, but I don't agree.

12 **Listen to the instructions and colour the pictures.**

a)

b)

c)

d)

Week 3 Natural wonders of the world

1 **Draw a line from each natural wonder to the country where it is found.**

Komodo National Park •   • Brazil

Table Mountain •   • Philippines

Ha Long Bay •   • South Africa

Iguazu Falls •   • Vietnam

Jejudo •   • Argentina

Underground River •   • South Korea

Amazon River •   • Indonesia

2 **Would you like to go to the places on pages 35–37 in your Student's Resource Book? Make questions using the words. Use the example to help you.**

Example: the Komodo National Park / see the dragons?

Would you like to go to the Komodo National Park to see the dragons?

Yes, please. / No, thank you.

a) Iguazu / visit the waterfall?

Would you like to _____

Yes, please. / No, thank you.

b) Ha Long Bay / explore the islands?

Would you like _____

Yes, please. / No, thank you.

c) Amazon river / see the rainforest?

Would you _____

Yes, please. / No, thank you.

d) Jejudo / climb the volcano?

_____

Yes, please. / No, thank you.

Now answer the questions, using 'Yes, please' or 'No, thank you'.

3 **Draw a line to match the beginning of each sentence with a suitable ending.**

a) She dances •   • to keep fit.

b) He goes to the library •   • to visit his grandparents.

c) They travel •   • to help her dad.

d) Lee has flown to Scotland •   • to find out about new places.

e) Josie is going to wash the car •   • to study for his exams.

4 **Correct the mistakes in the sentences. Rewrite the sentences correctly.**

a) We visited Ha Long Bay next month.

_____

b) We will sail down the Amazon River yesterday.

_____

c) Five thousand people visited the Komodo National Park tomorrow.

_____

_____

5 **Write your own sentences using: _last night, next year, today._**

a) last night: _____

_____

b) next year: _____

_____

c) today: _____

_____

6 **Read Li's scrapbook on pages 35–37 of the Student's Resource Book again. Complete these sentences about her trip.**

a) We rode on a boat _____.

b) You can see more than 1 430 different plants _____.

c) The Amazon River flows _____.

d) Many fishermen live _____.

e) The Iguazu Falls are _____.

f) Jejudo is a _____.

7 **Unscramble the letters and write the words.**

a) Have you ever been to **ouSth firAca** _____?

b) Have you ever had a ride in a cable **rac** _____?

c) Have you ever climbed a **notmunai** _____?

8 **Circle the correct answer on each card.**

a) The Komodo National Park is in:	**b)** Table Mountain is in:
• South Africa	• South Africa
• Vietnam	• Vietnam
• Indonesia	• Indonesia

c) Ha Long Bay is in:

• South Africa

• Vietnam

• Indonesia

9 **Hema's brother Yusuf went on a trip to Table Mountain. Write suitable words to complete their conversation.**

Hema: Hello Yusuf. What did you do _____?

Yusuf: Hi! I went up Table Mountain this _____.

Hema: That _____ dangerous.

Yusuf: No, it was lots of fun! I went up the mountain _____ a cable car.

Hema: _____ did you see?

Yusuf: I saw lots of rocks and plants on the way _____.

Hema: What _____ did you get back?

Yusuf: I got back an hour _____.

Hema: What are you going to do _____?

Yusuf: I'm _____ to swim in the sea.

10 **Write the missing words so that these sentences make sense. Choose the words from the box. You will need to use some of the words more than once.**

after	before	so	when

a) Clouds cover Table Mountain _____ the wind blows.

b) We cannot go up Table Mountain _____ the wind blows.

c) The mountain is very steep, _____ we'll take a cable car to get to the top.

d) I got a fright _____ a Komodo dragon lizard walked towards me.

e) The tour finished _____ we saw the Komodo dragon lizards.

f) You hear an echo _____ you shout inside a cave.

g) You have to buy a ticket _____ you can ride on a boat down the Amazon River.

11 Write the missing prepositions.

a) There are over 1 000 small islands _____ Ha Long Bay.

b) Clouds cover the top _____ Table Mountain.

c) The underground river flows _____ a large cave in the Philippines.

d) We went diving _____ the Komodo National Park.

e) The Iguazu Falls are found _____ Brazil and Argentina.

f) There are 360 small volcanoes _____ Jejudo.

12 Answer these questions. Use the words 'yes' or 'no' in your answers.

a) Are there more than 1 430 different plants on Table Mountain?

_____

b) Are there more than 1 900 small islands in Ha Long Bay?

_____

c) Are the Iguazu Falls made up of 280 separate waterfalls?

_____

d) Are there 360 smaller volcanoes around Jejudo?

_____

13 Unscramble the words to make sentences. Write the sentences correctly with capital letters and full stops.

a) komodo saw lizard a we dragon

_____

b) a amazon flows river rainforest through the

_____

Unit 6 The Olympic Games

Week 1 The Olympics in ancient times

1 **Match each picture to its meaning.**

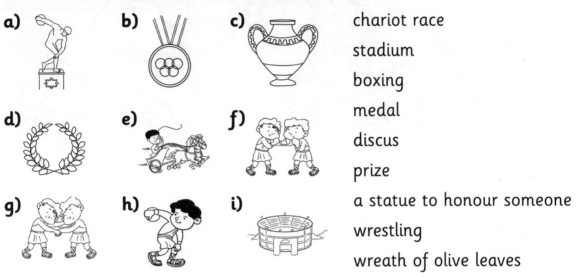

a)

b)

c)

chariot race

stadium

boxing

medal

d)

e)

f)

discus

prize

g)

h)

i)

a statue to honour someone

wrestling

wreath of olive leaves

2 **It is possible to make over 850 English words using the letters in the words 'ancient games'. For example, the words *act*, *ant*, *meets* and *engines*. With a partner see if you can make 30 words. Each word must have at least three letters.**

1	11	21
2	12	22
3	13	23
4	14	24
5	15	25
6	16	26
7	17	27
8	18	28
9	19	29
10	20	30

3 Look at the picture. Complete the activities.

a) Draw a green circle around the fastest chariot racer.

b) Draw a red circle around the slowest chariot racer.

c) Write the missing words in the following sentences about chariot racing. Choose words from the box.

best   bravest   fastest   most   other   proud   slowest

Chariot racing was one of the _____ exciting events at the Olympics. Only the _____ racer won an olive wreath. The _____ racers won nothing at all. Nobody wanted to be the _____ racer. They all wanted to be the fastest.

The horses were chosen for their strength and speed. Only the _____ horses were chosen.

The chariot drivers were chosen for their bravery. Only the _____ drivers were chosen.

The chariot drivers felt very _____ to participate in the event.

4 Choose the correct answer for each question.

1 Where were the first Olympics held?

a) The Colosseum.

b) Olympia.

2 When were the first Olympics held?

a) 667 BCE.

b) 776 BCE.

3 What was the only event in the first Olympic Games?

a) A short running race.

b) A marathon.

4 Who was allowed to participate in the games?

a) Everyone.

b) Only men who spoke Greek.

5 How were the winners of events rewarded?

a) They were given a medal.

b) They were given an olive wreath.

6 How can we tell that the Olympic Games were valued by the Greeks?

a) Women could not participate.

b) The Greeks stopped fighting a month before the Games.

7 Who won the running races for four games in a row?

a) Kyniska of Sparta.

b) Leonidas of Rhodes.

5 **Look at the pictures carefully. Write a sentence describing what is happening in each picture.**

> The ancient Greeks did not have cameras, so artists painted pictures of the Olympics on jars and vases.

a)

The men are _____

_____ .

b) The man _____

_____ .

c)

_____

_____ .

d) _____

_____ .

6 **Choose one of your sentences and write it in a more interesting way by adding adjectives and adverbs.**

_____

_____

7 **Read the conversation between two friends who are talking about the Olympic Games. Choose the best words to complete their conversation.**

Dimitros: The chariot race was very exciting!

Iris: All the horses ran (fast / faster), but Kyniska's horses ran (fast / faster).

Dimitros: Yes, her horses ran (the fastest / the fast) and won the race.

Iris: I bet the crowd cheered (loud / loudly)!

Dimitros: The people near me cheered (more loudly / loudest) than the others. They cheered the (loudly / loudest)!

Iris: I think the athletes have to train very (harder / hard), but the best athlete trains (the hardest / the harder)!

Dimitros: All the athletes train (the hardest / hard), but the winner can train a little less (hard / hardest) than the others!

Iris: The athletes who take part in the Games run or fight (the best / well) in all of Greece. They have taken part (more successful / successfully) in other competitions and have won them. But the Olympics are important because they show us who does the sport (the most successfully / more successfully). These are the champions of all of Greece!

8 **Choose words from each column to build five different sentences. Write your sentences below the table.**

The men	has	run	to	the stadium.
The athletes	have	compete	in	the arena.
The chariot racers		raced	around	the track.
		boxed		the ring.
The man				the Games.
The wrestler				

1: _____

2: _____

3: _____

4: _____

5: _____

9 **The winner of an Olympic event is talking. Complete the sentences for them.**

a) When you want to be the best, you have to _____.

b) When you do not train hard, you _____.

c) Before I race, I _____.

d) Before I sleep, I _____.

e) After I finish a race, I _____.

f) After I finish training, I _____.

Week 2 From ancient to modern

Adverbs of frequency tell us how often something is done. For example, I **always** do my homework and I **never** go to bed late. 'Always' tells us that this person does homework every time it is given and that they do not go to bed late at all. 'Never' means the same as 'not ever'.

1   **Work in pairs. Discuss the words in the box and make sure you know what each one means. Then put them in the correct place on the diagram.**

always   never   often   sometimes   usually

|——————————————————————|

|----------|----------|----------|----------|

2   **Read the conversation between two Olympic cyclists. Read the clues at the end of each sentence and fill in an adverb of frequency to complete each sentence.**

Jan: I _____ warm up before I ride. (He does this every time.)

Alexander: So do I. I _____ ride before my muscles are stretched and warm. (He does not do this at all.)

Jan: I _____ go to bed early before a race. (He does this almost every time.)

Alexander: I _____ don't sleep well before a race. (This happens more times than it doesn't happen.)

Jan: _____, I sleep well, but not always. (This happens some of the time.)

3 **Choose the correct adverbs to complete the sentences.**

a) Sonia has (always / already) won three medals! Let's see if she can win her fourth.

b) Are the competitors ready for the next race, (yet / ever)?

c) Have you (ever / never) run faster than her?

d) Hurry up! The race has (always / already) started. You'll miss it.

e) I have (ever / always) wanted to compete in the Olympics. It's my dream.

f) I don't (ever / never) want to trip and fall when I'm skating.

g) Don (yet / never) forgets to thank the rest of the team when he wins. He remembers every time.

h) Our team hasn't won any games (yet / never).

4 **Circle the correct word in each sentence.**

a) The runner who comes third in a race is (slow / slower / the slowest) than the runner who comes second.

b) The swimmer who comes first in a race is (fast / faster / the fastest) swimmer of them all.

c) The athlete who wins all her races is the (good / better / best) athlete.

d) The team that doesn't play well together will get a (bad / worse / worst) score than the others.

5 **Choose words from the box to complete these sentences.**

better	faster	first	least	most	third

a) The runner who came first in her race is _____ than the runner who came second.

b) The swimmer who came second in the race is slower than the swimmer who came _____.

c) The skier who finishes _____ is the winner.

d) The gymnast with the _____ points is the winner.

e) The gymnast who wins a bronze medal is _____ than the gymnast who is placed fourth.

6 **Write a paragraph to describe a photograph of people watching a sporting event. Try to include as many words from the box as you can. Don't forget to check your work for correct spelling and punctuation.**

anyone	anything	everyone	everything
no one	nothing	someone	something

_____

_____

_____

_____

_____

7 **Where do these events take place? Use the words from the box and the example to help you.**

court	ice rink	pitch	road	track	water

Example: Swimmers compete <u>in the pool.</u>

a) Cyclists ride _____.

b) Sprinters run _____.

c) Hockey matches are played _____.

d) Tennis matches are played _____.

e) Figure skating takes place _____.

f) Canoeists paddle _____.

8 **Find the names of eight sports in the word ribbon. Write the names of the sports on the medals.**

crickettennisswimminghockeydivingfencingboxingrunning

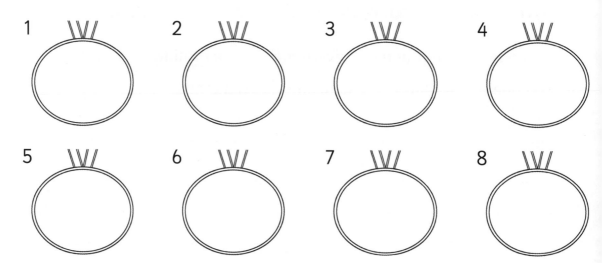

9 **Find and circle the word that doesn't fit in each set.**

a) run   sprint   walk

b) dance   jump   leap

c) throw   toss   miss

d) jog   run   march

e) pass   throw   catch

f) ride   cycle   swim

10 **Read the sentences. Circle the nouns and underline the adjectives in each sentence.**

a) The Canadian team wore red jerseys.

b) The fastest runner was the one in the inside lane.

c) The tall sprinter was wearing gold shoes.

d) The fastest swimmer was wearing a blue cap.

e) The huge Olympic torch has a bright orange flame.

f) The most successful Olympian won twenty-two Olympic medals.

Week 3 Going for gold!

1 **Complete the notes with information from Student's Resource Book page 42.**

Name: _Usain Bolt_

Country: _____

Qualities: _____

Gold medals (when?): _____

Other sporting achievements: _____

_____

2 **Are these facts or opinions? Do you agree with them? Tell your partner why or why not.**

a) Usain Bolt is the best runner in the world.

b) Anyone can compete in the Olympic Games.

c) Everyone likes watching sport.

d) Millions of people watch the Olympic Games on TV.

e) Swimming is more fun than running.

3 **Write 'was' or 'were' to complete each sentence.**

a) The swimmer _____ warming up in the pool.

b) Some swimmers _____ not in the pool yet.

c) We _____ cheering for Usain Bolt.

d) Each gymnast _____ wearing a tracksuit.

e) All of the gymnasts _____ young and fit.

f) I _____ trying to watch the games on TV.

4 **Read this conversation between Usain Bolt and his coach. Choose words from the box to complete the sentences. You need to use some words more than once.**

| any | anything | nothing | some | something |

Usain: Do you have _____ tips for me?

Coach: I do have _____ ideas to help you run faster.

Usain : I'll do _____ you say. I want to be the best!

Coach: Have you done _____ warm up laps?

Usain : I've done _____ but not enough.

Coach: Let me tell you _____. If you don't warm up, you'll get cramp, and that is not _____ you want!

Usain : I know. _____ you say is new to me. Let me do _____ more laps before we plan my next victory!

5 **Match the beginning of each sentence to a suitable ending. Then write the questions they answer.**

a) We go to the gym • • to make them train harder.

b) Olympic athletes train hard • • to stay healthy.

c) We need to eat fresh fruit • • to get fit.

d) The coach shouted at the athletes • • to win their races.

a) _____

b) _____

c) _____

d) _____

6 **Choose the correct words in the brackets to complete the gaps in the sentences. The first one has been done for you.**

a) We all did ___*badly*___ in the test, but I did ___*the worst*___. (badly / the worst)

b) All the birds here sing _____, but those blue birds over there are singing _____. (beautifully / the most beautifully)

c) Jonas danced _____ at the party. In fact, he danced _____ of all the people there. (happily / the most happily)

d) The fans cheered _____, but then they cheered _____ when their team was losing! (noisily / less noisily)

e) That girl over there plays football very _____. She's playing _____ than the other people in her team. (well / better)

f) Bruce scored _____ in the competition, but I don't think he played _____ than some of the other players. (worse / the worst)

g) Usain ran _____ in the race, even though the other runners were trying to run _____. (faster / the fastest)

7   Read the questions. Answer in complete sentences.

a) Will an athlete win for coming first in a race at the Olympic Games?

_____

b) Will athletes train for the Olympic Games?

_____

c) Will athletes feel happy if they get beaten in a race?

_____

d) What will happen if an athlete does not do warm ups?

_____

e) What will happen if an athlete cheats?

_____

f) What will happen when an athlete wins a race?

_____

g) What will happen when an athlete does not train?

_____

h) How will athletes feel when they retire?

_____

i) How will an athlete feel if they win all their races?

_____

j) How will an athlete feel if they lose their races?

_____

8 **Sadia has written a list of things that happened when she went to watch skeleton sledding at the Olympics but she hasn't put it in the correct order. Put it in the correct order and write a paragraph to describe what happened. Don't forget to add some words to connect the sentences.**

On the way home we bought T-shirts.

We went to watch skeleton sledding at the Olympics.

She asked us for our tickets.

We got there, we spoke to the lady at the entrance.

We got home, my mum wanted to watch the event again on TV.

I took my camera with me.

_____

_____

_____

_____

_____

_____

_____

_____

9 **The information in the box gives you details of a family's trip to watch swimming at the Olympic Games. Use the information to write a paragraph about the trip. Don't forget to check your paragraph when you have finished writing.**

Arrived at 12.30 p.m. and left at 4.30 p.m. We caught a train to the stadium. My mum bought the tickets online a week before we went. We had to wait to get into the stadium. We had ice cream and fruit at 3 o'clock. The races were exciting. I took lots of photographs. The races finished at 4.30 p.m.

_____

_____

_____

_____

_____

_____

_____

_____

_____

10 **Read the information in your Student's Resource Book again.**

Describe three unusual Olympic events.

Event 1: _____

Event 2: _____

Event 3: _____

Unit 7 Communicating with others

Week 1 Our eyes and ears

1   Look at the pictures. Say the name of each food. Circle the foods you like best.

2   Look at the pictures of things that you can smell. Tick the things you would not like to smell.

3   Write the name of each body part.

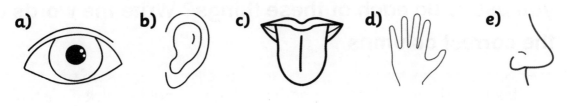

a)   b)   c)   d)   e)

_____   _____   _____   _____   _____

4   Complete the sentences.

a)   We use our eyes to _____.

b)   We use our ears to _____.

c)   We use our nose to _____.

d)   We use our fingers to _____.

e)   We use our tongue to _____.

5   Are the statements true or false?

a)   Everybody has senses. _____

b)   The sense organs are connected to the spine. _____

c)   Humans can see in colour. _____

d)   Our ears help us to balance. _____

Talk about these questions in your group.

Which do you think is our most important sense? Why?

Which do you think is our least important sense? Why?

If you could improve one of your senses, which one would it be? Why?

Some animals have a sense of smell that is 10,000 times better than ours. What do you think it would be like if you could smell that well?

6 **Read the words in the box. Which sense organ would you use to do each of these things? Write the words in the correct columns.**

blink	chew	grab	handle	hear	hold	lick	listen
point	smell	sniff	stare	stroke	touch	watch	

Eyes (Sight)	Ears (Hearing)	Nose (Smell)	Mouth and tongue (Taste)	Hands (Touch)

7 **Write your answers to these questions.**

a) What is the most beautiful thing you have ever seen?

_____

b) What is the most wonderful smell?

_____

c) What is the best taste in the world?

_____

d) What is your favourite sound?

_____

e) What is the softest thing you've ever touched?

_____

8 **Choose the correct words in each sentence. Cross out the incorrect words.**

a) When you spin around, (lots of / much) messages from your eyes and ears are sent to your brain.

b) Your skin contains (much / lots of) nerve endings.

c) Your pupil is small to stop too (much / many) light getting in and damaging your eye.

d) Once people reach their 20s, they're unable to hear as (much / many) sounds.

e) The surface of your tongue is covered in (much / lots of) tiny bumps.

f) (Each / Every) of our senses sends millions of messages to our brain in a second.

g) When there is only (a little / few) light, humans can only see in black and white.

9 **Pretend you are in the picture. Answer the questions.**

a) How many people can you see? _____

b) Is the baby crying loudly or softly? _____

c) Do the flowers feel prickly or soft? _____

10 **What do you think the mother is saying to her son in the picture on page 109? Underline the sentence that fits the conversation.**

    a) **Mum, the baby is crying.**

        I know. I can feel her. / I know. I can hear her.

    b) **What must I do?**

        Look to see if her bottle is empty. / Look to feel if her bottle is empty.

    c) **The baby won't drink her bottle.**

        Perhaps she is tired. / Perhaps she doesn't like the taste of her juice.

    d) **What else can I do?**

        Give the baby her soft blanket. / Give the baby her scratchy blanket.

11 **Complete these sentences.**

I like the sound of _____ more than the sound of _____.

I like the taste of _____ more than the taste of _____.

I like the feel of _____ more than the feel of _____.

I like the smell of _____ more than the smell of _____.

12 **Write a paragraph about what you see, hear, smell, taste and feel when you first wake up.**

_____

_____

_____

_____

_____

_____

_____

13 Unscramble the words and write each sentence.

a) different We of can sounds. types hear

_____

_____

b) of Smells can danger. us warn

_____

_____

c) can Your softness the feel of rabbit's a fingertips fur.

_____

_____

14 Circle the correct words in each sentence.

a) A feather feels (soft / softer) than a rock.

b) An ice cube feels (cold / colder) when you touch it.

c) My cheek is (soft / softer / softest), my sweater is (soft / softer / softest) than my cheek, but a flower is the (soft / softer / softest) of all.

d) The tap water is (cold / colder / coldest), the milkshake is (cold / colder / coldest), but the ice cream is the (cold / colder / coldest).

15 Write the correct form of the words in brackets.

a) Yesterday, Francis _____ (see) a tiny kitten.

b) Yesterday, Mae _____ (hear) a small bird tweet.

c) Yesterday, I _____ (go) to the shops.

d) I _____ (feel) cold last night.

Week 2 Braille

1 Charlie is blind. His mother takes him shopping with her so he can learn more about the world. Read what they do when they go shopping together. Take note of how Charlie uses his other senses.

Charlie loves to go shopping with his mum. He likes to touch all the fruit and vegetables even if his mum doesn't buy anything. Just think about it – when he touches a real pineapple, he learns that pineapples are spiky!

Charlie's mum talks to him about all the things in the shop. When they walk past the bakery section, Charlie learns what freshly baked bread smells like. When they walk past the deli section, Charlie learns to tell the difference between the types of cheese on sale, just by smelling them! In the aisles, Charlie touches cans and boxes and enjoys shaking them – have you ever noticed that a box of pasta sounds very different to a box of rice or breakfast cereal?

2 Unscramble the names of some of the things Charlie learned about when he went shopping. Write the words correctly.

berad   elcare   spata   hecese

_____   _____   _____   _____

3 Circle the correct word in each sentence.

a) When Charlie touched a plum, he learned that plums are (smooth / rough).

b) After Charlie touched a bird, he knew that feathers are (spiky / soft).

c) Before Charlie touched a kitten, he didn't know that fur is (soft / sticky).

d) When Charlie touched a rose bush, he discovered that thorns are (soft / spiky).

4 Ice feels cold, cooked food feels hot. The words 'cold' and 'hot' are opposites. Find a word that means the opposite of each word in the list.

a) big   _____

b) rough   _____

c) hard   _____

d) heavy   _____

e) loose   _____

f) short   _____

g) same   _____

h) wet   _____

i) sticky   _____

5 **Complete the sentences.**

a) When Charlie touches an ice cube, he learns that _____

_____.

b) When Charlie touches an apple, he learns that _____

_____.

c) When Charlie touched a sweater, he learned _____

_____.

6 **Circle the best word in each sentence.**

a) I don't want to eat a lemon because it tastes (sour / sweet).

b) I don't want to touch a cactus because it's too (prickly / smooth).

c) I don't want to smell the rotten food because it smells (awful / good)

7 **Choose the correct answer. Circle the letter.**

1 What is a table made from?

a) Wood

b) Bricks

c) Water

2 What does a table feel like?

a) Rough

b) Old

c) Smooth

3 What is a sweater made from?

a) Wood

b) Wool

c) Water

4 What does a sweater feel like?

a) Hard

b) Dirty

c) Soft

8 **Circle the items below that feel soft when you touch them. Write a word to describe how the other items would feel.**

a)    b)   c)    d)    e)

_____   _____   _____   _____   _____

9 **Draw a line to match the beginning of each sentence to its ending.**

Charlie cannot see, so ●   ● he wants to cross the road.

Charlie has to ask for help when ●   ● we see a blind person trying to cross the road.

We must always help when ●   ● where he is going.

A blind person has to feel ●   ● he can get hurt easily.

10 Circle the correct word in each sentence.

a) Our sight is precious, (so / where) we must always protect our eyes from the sun.

b) Our eyes hurt (so / when) we look at the sun.

c) We need to wear a hat (when / so) we go into the sun.

d) We must always look (after / where) we're going.

11 Write 'Before', 'After' or 'When' in each sentence.

a) _____ we cross the road, we must check that the road is clear.

b) _____ we do our homework, we can play.

c) _____ you ask for help, try and figure out the answer yourself.

d) _____ you get cross, take a deep breath.

e) _____ we go to the park, we catch the bus.

f) _____ I went to bed, I brushed my teeth.

g) _____ they saw the film, they bought some pizza on the way home.

h) _____ Emre tasted the fruit, he discovered he liked it.

12 **Listen to the information about Morse code and then complete the paragraph using words from the box.**

| also | as | be | Before | by | for | of | on | which |

Morse code was invented _____ Samuel Finley Morse. He was born _____ 27 April, 1791. _____ he invented Morse code, he worked as an inventor and artist.

Morse Code is a system in _____ letters are represented _____ dots and dashes.

The dots are the short sounds and are also known _____ dits.

The dashes are the long sounds and are _____ known _____ dahs. Because you can also tap out the dots and dashes, Morse code can _____ both seen and heard.

The first message in Morse code was sent _____ 24 May, 1844. It travelled a distance _____ nearly 65 kilometres.

The signal _____ help is S.O.S. This can be sent _____ Morse code. People can send Morse code _____ flickering lights. Morse code is still used _____ communication today.

13 **Use the code to work out what the message says.**

A	B	C	D	E	F	G	H	I	J	K	L	M
1	2	3	4	5	6	7	8	9	10	11	12	13
N	O	P	Q	R	S	T	U	V	W	X	Y	Z
14	15	16	17	18	19	20	21	22	23	24	25	26

8　1　22　5　1　7　18　5　1　20　4　1　25!

Week 3 Helen Keller

1 **Answer these questions about Helen Keller. Then write your own questions.**

a) When was she born? _____

b) When did she get sick? _____

c) When did she learn her first word from Anne Sullivan?

_____

d) _____

e) _____

2 **Number the sentences to show their correct order.**

a) [ ] Helen finished college.

b) [ ] Helen got sick.

c) [ ] Helen was born.

d) [ ] Helen began making speeches.

e) [ ] Helen wrote a book.

3 **Read the statements. If the statement is true, tick the box. If it is false, make an X inside the box.**

a) Helen was happy before she learned to communicate. [ ]

b) Helen wanted to help deaf and blind people. [ ]

c) Anne Sullivan helped Helen to communicate. [ ]

4 **Choose the right word to complete these questions. Then answer them with a partner.**

a) Could Helen see or hear (anything / something)?

b) Could Helen communicate with (anyone / something)?

c) Did Helen achieve (anything / someone) at college?

5 **Complete the sentences. Choose the missing words from the box.**

already	always	ever	never	yet

a) We haven't decided where we want to go on holiday _____.

b) I _____ go on holiday with my grandparents. They don't like to travel.

c) They have _____ been to that funpark. They loved it.

d) Has he _____ seen the film about the toys?

e) She _____ eats her supper at 9 o'clock and then she brushes her teeth.

f) Have you had your lunch, _____?

g) They have _____ ridden a camel, but they want to try it.

h) Do you have a book I can read? I've _____ read this one.

i) You _____ go to interesting places. Don't you?

j) We _____ drop rubbish on the pavement. Do we?

6 **Write your own sentences.**

a) I always _____

_____.

b) I haven't _____

_____ yet.

c) I have already. _____

_____.

7 **Read the conversation between Helen Keller's parents and a doctor. Write 'might', 'may' or 'could' to complete the sentences.**

Doctor: Your daughter is very ill.

Mrs Keller: _____ she lose her sight?

Doctor: Yes, she _____.

Mrs Keller: _____ she lose her hearing?

Doctor: Yes, she _____.

Mrs Keller: Will she be able to communicate?

Doctor: She _____, but I don't think so.

8 **Read the sentences and choose the right word.**

a) He (may / could) quickly see the answer to the maths problem.

b) We (might / could) be able to finish our homework before dinner if we start now!

c) (Might / May) she be top of the class if she studies hard? Yes, she (might / could).

d) I (could / might) not pass the exam if I don't study hard.

e) (Might / May) we speak to the Head Teacher please?

f) She (might / could) not be able to go on the school trip to the museum because she isn't feeling very well.

g) He (may / could) not arrive in time because all the trains are late today.

9 Rewrite the following sentences as if the action is taking place right now.

a) The doctor gave her medicine.

_____

b) Her parents tried to help her.

_____

c) Anne Sullivan came to stay with the family.

_____

d) She taught Helen.

_____

e) Helen learned to spell.

_____

10 Complete the paragraphs with the correct past form of the verbs in brackets.

When Helen was a little girl, she _____ (is) angry because she _____ (cannot) communicate with her family. When she was angry, she _____ (kick) and _____ (scream). But she _____ (keep) trying and _____ (tell) her family things by making signs. For example, she _____ (shiver) when she was cold.

After Ann Sullivan arrived, she _____ (work) hard every day to help Helen to learn to read, write and speak. Ann went with Helen to college and _____ (help) Helen with her work there.

11 Who are these people? Unscramble the words and write their names on the lines.

leehn klleer _____

nnea aluislvn _____

12 Use the clues to complete the crossword puzzle.

Across

1 _____ Keller wanted to help people communicate.

2 Helen used this to read books.

3 Anne _____ became her teacher and friend.

4 If you are _____, you cannot hear.

Down

5 Helen _____ was born in 1880.

6 _____ Sullivan helped Helen Keller communicate with the world.

7 If you are _____, you cannot see.

8 Another word for feeling 'sick'.

Unit 8 Thoughts, feelings and opinions

Week 1 Fashion forward!

1 **Answer the questions about Jonathan's shopping trip.**

a) Was his mother excited to go shopping?

_____

b) Why did Jonathan not like the blue jumper?

_____

c) Why did Jonathan not buy the yellow trousers?

_____

d) What did Jonathan make with the sewing machine?

_____

2 **Choose and circle the correct words in each sentence.**

a) Mum (has to / had to) go to work yesterday afternoon.

b) Today Jonathan (has to / had to) buy new clothes for school.

c) Yesterday, Mum (has to / had to) ask Gran for help.

d) Gran (has to / had to) help Jonathan while he is learning to sew.

3 **Complete this paragraph.**

Jonathan's favourite item of clothing is his _____

because _____. He wears this item

when he goes to _____.

He wears this item when the weather is _____.

4 Design an imaginary outfit for yourself on top of the figure. Use your favourite colours and patterns.

Now, write a paragraph describing your outfit. Remember to include information about the colours, patterns and textures you have chosen.

I am wearing

_____

_____

_____

_____

Read your paragraph aloud to your partner. Listen to their paragraph, and ask questions about their outfit. Have you left any details out of your description?

5 Check your paragraph. Check spelling and punctuation. Rewrite your paragraph and add the missing details you thought about in activity 4.

_____

_____

_____

6   Complete the paragraphs. Don't forget the punctuation.

I like to wear the colour _____ because

_____

My least favourite type of clothing is _____ I

like to wear _____ I don't like to wear

_____ I like shopping because

_____ I don't like shopping because

_____

7   Listen to the fun fashion facts. Choose words from the box to fill the gaps.

| collect   dress   famous   foot   materials   popular   throw |

a)   The T-shirt is a very _____ piece of clothing.

b)   Napoleon was a _____ army leader who put buttons on uniform sleeves to stop soldiers wiping their noses on them.

c)   Most clothes are made with _____ like cotton or polyester.

d)   Grabatologists _____ ties.

e)   Marilyn Monroe's _____ was covered in 6 000 rhinestones.

f)   Many people have one _____ that is bigger than the other one.

g)   Astronauts _____ their clothes into space.

8 **Choose words from each column and make five different sentences to show what you remember about the story in the Student's Resource Book. Use the example to help you.**

Jonathan is the boy	who	wanted to go shopping
There is the fabric	that	is very expensive
Mum is the woman	which	they sell clothes?
Is that the place		wanted to teach him to sew
Here is the grandmother		is very tired
		became a T-shirt
		has a hole in it?

Example: *Jonathan is the boy who wanted to go shopping.*

1: _____

_____

2: _____

_____

3: _____

_____

4: _____

_____

5: _____

_____

9 **Read the descriptions below the boxes. Draw and colour in the fabric pattern in the box.**

This fabric looks like clouds in the sky.	This fabric looks like a stormy sea.
This fabric looks like a rainbow.	This fabric looks like grass.

10 **Draw and colour in two more fabric patterns. Then swap your drawings with a partner. Fill in the missing words under their drawings.**

This fabric looks like _____	This fabric looks like _____

11 **Jonathan and his friend Ben are talking about a new clothes shop. Fill the gaps in the conversation with 'like' or 'about'.**

Ben: Did you hear _____ the new shop?

Jonathan: Yes. It's just _____ the big one on the high street, but it's less expensive.

Ben: My sister told me _____ it. They have clothes that look _____ the latest designs.

Jonathan: I bought my sneakers from there.

Ben: Really? They look _____ mine.

Jonathan: Yes, but I think I paid less!

12 What is your favourite story? Complete the paragraph.

My favourite story is _____. It is from a film/book. My favourite character in the story is _____ because _____ _____. The story is about _____

_____.

I like this story because _____.

13 Listen to your partner's description. Write a message to a friend about what your partner has told you.

Hi! How are you?

Today in school, I talked to _____ about their favourite story and I want to tell you about it.

Their favourite story is _____. It is from a film/book. Their favourite character in the story is

_____ because _____.

The story is about _____.

They like it because _____.

That's all for now!

14 Jonathan and his friend Ben are out shopping. Complete their conversation with the words in the box.

any   anything   nothing   some   something

Ben: Is there _____ we can buy in this shop?

Jonathan: No, there's _____ I want to buy.

Ben: Are there any T-shirts?

Jonathan: Yes there are _____, but I don't like the colours.

Ben: Are there any sneakers?

Jonathan: No, there aren't _____.

Ben: Well, I need to buy _____ for my sister's birthday, so I'm going to look!

Week 2 A new school

1 **Look at the diary entry on page 52 of the Student's Resource Book and complete the sentences.**

a) This diary entry is about _____.

b) Jihu is good at _____.

c) Jia misses _____.

d) Jia likes to _____.

2 **The pictures tell a story about Jia's first day at her new school. Use the pictures to complete the paragraph.**

a)

b)

c)

It was a bad day for Jia. First, _____

_____.

Then, _____

_____.

Finally, _____

_____.

Starting at a new school is _____.

3 **Choose words from the box to complete the sentences.**

| yet   ever   already   always   soon   never |

a) Mum asks Jia if she has joined a school club _____.

b) Jia says, "Mum, will we _____ go back to our old school?"

c) Mum says that Jia can visit Eun _____.

d) Jihu has _____ made friends at school.

e) Jia _____ reads comics instead of listening in class.

f) Jia has _____ played football before.

4 **Listen. Then answer the questions.**

a) Jihu plays football, doesn't he?

_____

b) Jia tripped, didn't she?

_____

c) The teacher shouted, didn't she?

_____

d) Jihu isn't shy, is he?

_____

e) Mum doesn't understand, does she?

_____

5 **Match the two parts to finish the questions. Then write the complete questions.**

The dance is on Friday,	can't you?
You can do hip hop dance,	aren't they?
You like films,	isn't he?
Comics are exciting,	is she?
She isn't good at football,	don't you?
Your brother is at the same school,	isn't it?
You don't study English,	can he?
He can't ride a bike,	do you?

a) The dance is on Friday, _____

b) You can do hip hop dance, _____

c) You like films, _____

d) Comics are exciting, _____

e) She isn't good at football, _____

f) Your brother is at the same school, _____

g You don't study English, _____

h) He can't ride a bike, _____

6 **Jia is talking about her friend Eun. Complete the sentences with the correct past form of the verbs in brackets.**

When I was at my old school, I _____ (go) to a music club with my friend, Eun. We _____ (sing) traditional songs. In break time we _____ (read) comics together and _____ (draw) pictures of the best characters. At the weekends, we _____ (buy) the newest comics and often _____ (watch) our favourite cartoons on TV.

7 **What advice can you give Jia to help her feel comfortable at her new school? Write a set of instructions for her.**

1: _____

2: _____

3: _____

4: _____

5: _____

8 **Imagine you are inviting Jia to your birthday party. Complete the dialogue.**

You: Hello, Jia!

Jia: Hello, _____!

You: I am having a birthday party this weekend. Would you like _____?

Jia: _____, please.

You: Great!

Jia: Would you like me to bring anything with me?

You: No, _____.

Jia: Okay. I am excited!

You: Would you like to come and sit with me? I have some crisps. Would you like one?

Jia: _____.

9 The head teacher is explaining all the different activities available at the school to Jia and Jihu. Look at the posters on page 53 of your Student's Resource Book. Complete the sentences, using the information about clubs and the words in brackets. Use the example filled in to help you.

What do you like to do?

Do you like dancing? You _could join the City Dance Academy._ (join)

Do you like playing football? You _____. (join)

Do you love to read comics? You _____. (join)

Do you enjoy watching and talking about films? You _____. (join)

What do you want to do?

Do you want to make new friends? You _____. (go to)

10 Choose a word from the box to complete the sentences. You can use the words more than once.

| that | where | who |

a) This is the projector _____ I use to show films.

b) I am looking for the student _____ is good at football.

c) Where is the teacher _____ wanted to talk to Jia?

d) That is the classroom _____ you will have English class.

11 Build a new classroom, using root words!

Root words are the core words that make up the foundation of longer words. For example:

	enjoying			
	enjoy			
joy				

In this example, 'joy' is the root word. We add "en-", and "-ing" to make the root word into different words.

Choose the letters from the boxes to add to the beginning or end of each root word to build more words. Write the new words in the three bricks. Try saying the words aloud.

a) **build** ☐ ☐ ☐

re- un- -ful -er -ing

b) **care** ☐ ☐ ☐

un- -less -ship -ful -er

c) **play** ☐ ☐ ☐

re- -er -ful -ly -ship

d) **friend** ☐ ☐ ☐

-er -ly -ship -less -ing

12 Look at Student's Resource Book page 52. Write a paragraph to explain how you think Jia feels, and why.

I think that Jia is _____, because _____

_____

_____

Week 3 What's in the news?

1 Read the paragraph about the reporter's interview with Sophia Wang. Choose the correct form of the verbs to complete it.

The reporter went (to interview / interviewing) Sophia before the show. The reporter (met/ was meeting) Sophia at her home. When he arrived, Sophia and her dad (were making/make) dumplings. He (tasted/was tasting) the dumplings that the judges liked so much. They were delicious!

The reporter (was ask/asked) Sophia about why she entered the competition. She said she (was washing/washed) dishes when she saw the advertisement for the competition. While she (was thinking/didn't think) about the competition, she didn't wash the pots very well! As they (talk/ were talking), Sophia's brother and mum walked into the kitchen too.

2 Imagine you are Sophia and you have just decided to enter a cooking competition. Write a short diary entry below explaining how you are feeling. Say why you have decided to enter the competition.

Date:_____

Dear diary,

_____

_____

_____

_____

_____

_____

3 **Rewrite this paragraph using the correct punctuation.**

yesterday the team was practising football out on the field the sun was shining and the weather was very hot joe alice and dev ran onto the pitch then the coach told them to kick the ball where was amal she ran too but tripped and fell poor amal

_____

_____

_____

_____

_____

4 **Circle the correct word to complete the sentences.**

a) Of all of his sports activities, he likes cricket (well / better / the best).

b) The boys ran fast, but the girls ran (fast / faster / fastest).

c) Anwar jumped high, Sally jumped higher and Sayeed jumped (high / higher / the highest).

d) The boy walks slowly, his father walks more slowly, but his grandfather walks (slowly / more slowly / the slowest).

5 **Finish these sentences. Use the example to help you.**

Example: He trains hard to _improve at cricket._

a) She reads books to _____

b) He goes to school to _____

c) She went to the shops to _____

d) I went home to _____

e) He plays cricket to _____

6 Complete the sentences about yourself. Use the example to help you.

Example: To do my shopping, I *go to the mall.*

a) To relax after school, I _____

b) To keep fit and healthy, I _____

c) To learn new things, I _____

d) To have fun, I _____

7 Read the information about the printing press and news.

The printing press is a machine that allows you to print many documents that look the same, in a short time.

Nobody knows when the first printing press was invented, but there are printed documents from China from as early as 868 CE.

The printing press became popular in Europe in the 1440s, when Johannes Gutenberg created another version of the printing press.

Before there were lots of printing presses, special people called scribes copied books by hand. Imagine how long it took to copy a single book! Books were very expensive because they took so long to make.

A printing press

A scribe

The printing press changed the world. It allowed us to print a lot of information and to spread it quickly for the first time. More people in society were able to see and buy printed materials. They were able to read books and the news. This meant that more people learned to read as well.

Today, people don't read so many printed books, magazines and newspapers because they read more online with electronic devices. Will printed pages disappear?

8 Imagine you can travel in time to speak to a scribe who is copying a book by hand. Write down five questions you would ask the scribe.

1: _____

2: _____

3: _____

4: _____

5: _____

9 The printing press changed how we shared information. Imagine what it would be like without the internet! Write down your five favourite things about the internet.

1: _____

2: _____

3: _____

4: _____

5: _____

10 Complete the blog post with your partner's list.

Today I talked to my partner about our favourite things about the internet.

My partner's name is _____

Their favourite things about the internet are:

1. _____

2. _____

3. _____

4. _____

5. _____

11 **Imagine you watched a sports event at your school yesterday. Write a short report about it.**

First, think about the questions in the box. You can include some of the answers in your report.

What was the event and who was playing or competing?

What was the weather like?

Who was watching?

Who won and what was the final result?

Did the spectators think the event was exciting or boring?

When you have finished, don't forget to check your writing for correct spelling and punctuation.

_____

_____

_____

_____

_____

_____

_____

_____

_____

_____

Unit 9 Let's go on holiday!

Week 1 A trip to the game reserve

1 **Label the picture with the names of the animals.**

2 **Groups of animals have special names. Match the group names to the animals.**

a herd of ●   ● lions

a pride of ●   ● birds

a band of ●   ● antelope

a flock of ●   ● monkeys

3 **Be creative! Write your own group names for these animals.**

a _____ of crocodiles

a _____ of snakes

4 **Choose the right words to complete this description of Anjali's holiday.**

Anjali (will go / went) to look at animals in a game reserve. When she was there, she (looked / look) through binoculars to try to find some animals. It (were / was) really great to see animals in the wild. She (loved / love) every minute of it. They (were / was) all really sad when the trip ended.

5 **Read these animal number problems. Work out the answers. You can use a calculator if you need to.**

a) One zebra has about 50 stripes. If you see three zebras on a game drive, about how many stripes would there be altogether? _____

b) If there are 100 zebras in a herd, how many stripes would there be? _____

c) An ostrich has two toes. How many toes would there be on 20 ostriches? _____

d) Giraffes have long, flexible tongues to grab leaves off the thorny acacia trees. If the average giraffe is able to eat 25 leaves off an acacia tree in one hour, how many acacia leaves would be eaten by seven giraffes in one hour? _____

e) If each monkey eats 20 berries, how many would five monkeys eat? _____

f) Three monkeys are eating berries. They eat a total of 60 berries. Two monkeys eat the same number of berries and the third one eats 10 berries. How many berries do the other two eat?

Make up an animal number problem of your own.

Swap with a partner and try to solve each other's problems.

6 Write down three places where you could find information about African animals.

_____ _____ _____

7 Choose an African animal and find out about it. Use the table to summarise your research.

African Animal Research	Size:
Name of animal:	Type of body covering:
Animal group (mammal, bird, reptile):	Food:
How it gets its food:	
How it is adapted to life in the wild:	

8 **Write the missing words.**

| fast | faster | fastest | slow | slower | slowest |

a) A wildebeest runs _____ than a tortoise, but it is
_____ than a cheetah.

b) The cheetah runs _____ than the wildebeest and the
tortoise. It is the _____ animal.

c) The tortoise is the _____ of all three animals. It is a
_____ animal.

9 **Imagine you are on safari in Africa looking at lions.**
Write a paragraph to describe what the lions are doing.
(Use your imagination!)

_____

_____

_____

_____

_____

_____

10 Read Anjali's diary and choose the correct answer.

1 What did Anjali do on Monday?

a) She brushed her teeth.

b) She went on a game drive.

c) She saw a lion.

2 What did Anjali do on Tuesday?

a) She went on a game drive and saw a zebra.

b) She went on a game drive and saw a lion.

c) She went on a game drive and saw a leopard.

3 Why did she spend most of Wednesday at the campsite?

a) It was too hot to go outside.

b) It was too cold and cloudy.

c) She wanted to swim.

11 Answer these questions in complete sentences.

a) What was the name of the tour guide?

_____

b) How many game drives did Anjali go on?

_____

c) Which animals did Anjali see on her holiday?

_____

12 Draw a picture of your favourite wild animal. Complete the sentence.

The _____ is my favourite

animal because _____

13 Read the clues. Write the animal's name.

a) This animal has a long tail. It can run fast and its coat is spotted. It is a _____.

b) This tall animal has a long neck. It also has a long tongue. It is a _____.

c) This animal swings in trees. It has a long, thin tail. It eats fruit and berries. It is a _____.

14 Unscramble the animal names and write them correctly.

a) ilno _____   **b)** aldepro _____

c) barze _____   **d)** faigrfe _____

15 Read the sentences and choose the right word.

a) It (may not / can't) be a lion because it has a very long neck. It (may / couldn't) be a giraffe.

b) The monkey (might / couldn't) climb the tree if it is hungry and wants to get the bananas!

c) It (couldn't / could) be a monkey, because it can climb a tree.

d) The elephant was very strong. It (could / may) carry three people on its back.

Week 2 Island fun

1 **Read the advertisement for a summer holiday on page 59 of the Student's Resource Book. Complete the sentences to say what you can do.**

a) _____ in the sun.

b) _____ fish.

c) _____ with dolphins.

d) _____ shells.

e) _____ new friends.

f) _____ in the clear blue sea.

2 **Use your own ideas to make sentences about a beach holiday. Use the examples to help you.**

a) I want to try swimming in the sea.

I want to try _____.

b) I am going to learn to scuba dive.

I am going to learn to _____.

c) When it starts to get hot, I'm going to sit in the shade.

When it starts to get cold, I'm going to _____.

d) Have you ever built a sand castle?

Have you ever _____?

e) It's fun to play here, isn't it?

It's fun to _____ here, isn't it?

f) I forgot to bring my bucket and spade.

I forgot to _____.

g) Could we buy some ice creams?

Could we buy some _____?

3   **List five things you can see in the picture.**

_____   _____

_____   _____

_____

4   **Complete the sentences to describe what is happening in the picture.**

a)   The man with _____ is reading the newspaper.

b)   The woman with _____ is reading a book.

c)   The children are _____.

d)   The family are sitting _____.

e)   The woman is sitting _____.

f)   The little boy is playing with _____.

5 Li is packing for a beach holiday. Draw lines to match each item to its name.

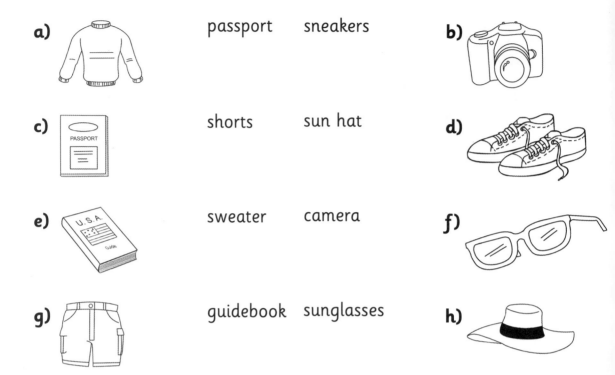

a)

passport   sneakers

b)

c)

shorts   sun hat

d)

e)

sweater   camera

f)

g)

guidebook   sunglasses

h)

6 On a piece of paper, draw two more items Li should pack for a beach holiday. Label them.

7 Choose the correct past verb forms to complete the paragraph.

My aunt and uncle (have lived / were living) in many different places. I (went / was going) to visit them while they (have lived / were living) in Spain. We (have been / went) to the beach nearly every day and often (spent / were spending) the whole day there. We (have swum /swam) in the sea and (were playing / played) games like football. Sometimes we (have visited / visited) somewhere interesting and (ate / have eaten) some tasty local food. I (was having/ had) a great time!

8 **Read the poem.**

> **Stay safe on the beach**
> Stay safe on the beach,
> And you can have fun.
> That's the rule
> For everyone.
> Don't swim alone
> and don't go too deep
> That's the rule
> We all must keep.
> Don't swim in the dark
> Swim during the day
> That's the rule
> We have to obey.

9 **Write two more instructions for staying safe on the beach.**

Rule 1: _____

Rule 2: _____

10 **Work with a partner. Write a conversation giving each other instructions for staying safe near water.**

_____

_____

_____

_____

11 Choose the correct words to complete these sentences.

a) We want (to swim / swimming) in the sea.

b) Yesterday, I managed (to build / building) a huge sandcastle!

c) When you are in the sea, avoid (to go / going) close to the rocks.

d) Oh no! I forgot (to bring / bringing) the sunblock.

e) Do you enjoy (to read / reading) on the beach?

f) I really dislike (to get / getting) sand in my shoes!

12 Imagine you are on a warm, sunny island with a lovely beach. Answer these questions about it.

a) What does the water feel like?

The water feels cool like _____.

b) What does the sand feel like?

The sand feels soft like _____.

c) What do the clouds look like?

The clouds look like _____.

13 Write a paragraph to describe the island on page 61 of the Student's Resource Book.

_____

_____

_____

_____

_____

_____

_____

14 **Where do you think these children are going?**
Circle items in the picture that tell you where
they are going.

Amit   Jose   Katja   John   Sanjita

15 **Answer these questions about the children in the**
picture.

a) Who is the tallest? _____

b) Who is the shortest? _____

c) Whose hair is longer than Katja's? _____

d) Who is shorter than Jose? _____

e) Is Sanjita taller than Amit? _____

f) Who is shorter: Amit or Katja? _____

g) Who looks the oldest? _____

16 **Write a postcard to your friend. Tell your friend about a day on the beach. Draw a picture to go on the front of your postcard.**

GREETINGS
from

17 Work in pairs. Find ten differences between these two pictures. Circle the things that are different in picture b.

a)   b)

18 Write sentences about things that are silly in the picture. Try to make them as interesting as possible. Say why they are silly.

a) _____

_____ .

b) _____

_____ .

c) _____

_____ .

Week 3 Sightseeing

1 **Learners are talking about their holidays. Read what they say. Complete the table.**

Carla: I'm going to Spain on Sunday. I am travelling by plane.

Raoul: I'm going to France next Friday. I am travelling by train.

Maria: I'm going on a bus trip to visit my family in Portugal.

Glenroy: I'm going on a boat cruise in Norway.

Learner	Where?	How?	When?
Carla	Spain	plane	Sunday
Raoul			
Maria			
Glenroy			

2 **Write the language that matches each country and the name of the capital city. Do research if you are not sure.**

Example: England _English_ _London_

a) Spain _____ _____

b) France _____ _____

c) Portugal _____ _____

d) Norway _____ _____

3 **Complete these sentences about your local area.**

I think the best _____ _____

My favourite _____ _____

I don't like _____ _____

4 **Write down three things visitors can do and one thing they cannot do in your area.**

_____

_____

_____

_____

_____

5 **Write about three things you are doing in the holidays.**

_____

_____

_____

_____

_____

_____

_____

_____

_____

_____

6 Answer the questions about the map.

a) Is the train station in the same road as the museum? Yes/No

b) Which is closer to the train station? The park / The police station

c) Which is further away from the train station? The theatre / The stadium

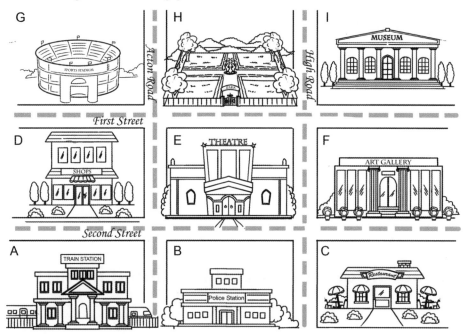

7 Write down three things you can do if you visit this city.

_____   _____   _____

8 Underline the correct part of the sentence.

The train station is (in front of / two blocks away) from the sports stadium.

The theatre is (in front of / behind) the police station.

The museum is (next to / behind) the park.

9 Write a clear set of directions for a tourist to help her get from the train station to the museum.

_____

_____

_____

10 Write a question to match each answer.

Question	Answer
	We are leaving next week.
	We are catching a train to the airport.
	I am staying with my aunt and uncle.
	I hope to go skiing and climbing.
	I think it will be cold and it might snow.

11 Imagine that a class from another country is coming to visit your country next week. Work in groups to plan a five day programme for their trip.

Programme for Class 4 visit		
	Things we are going to do and places we are going to visit	Transport arrangements
Day 1		
Day 2		
Day 3		
Day 4		
Day 5		

12 **Pretend that you are one of the children in the picture. Complete the sentences to describe your day.**

a) I am going to build a snowman that is larger than _____.

b) I am so cold. My ears feel like _____.

c) My fingers are blue from the cold. They look like _____.

d) The snow is covering the mountain. It looks like _____.

e) The mountain is the biggest I have ever seen. It is like a _____.

13 **Choose the right words to complete the sentences.**

a) This is the place (where / that) you can swim with dolphins.

b) Could you ask the person (who / where) is standing over there?

c) Where's the boat (who / that) leaves at 2 o'clock?

d) That's the large bag (who / which) I always take on holiday.

e) The name of the restaurant (who / where) we are meeting my parents is "Nico's".

f) Luis wants to buy a hat (that / where) protects his eyes.

g) They spoke to the man (which / who) sold them the tickets.

14 **Read the poems on page 63 of the Student's Resource Book again.**

Write all the words that end with —*ing* in the first column of the table. You should find sixteen different words.

Write the verb used to make the —*ing* word in the second column.

1	glittering	glitter
2		
3		
4		
5		
6		
7		
8		
9		
10		
11		
12		
13		
14		
15		
16		

15 **Choose a city that you know about. On a piece of paper, write your own poem using the same structure as the ones in the Student's Resource Book. Your poem can have seven or eight lines. Start with the name of the city.**

16 **This map shows some tourist attractions in London and how long it takes to walk from place to place. Answer the questions.**

① Tower Bridge 5 mins → ② Tower of London 20 mins → ③ St Paul's Cathedral 25 mins → ④ London Eye 10 mins → ⑤ Big Ben 5 mins → ⑥ Palace of Westminster 5 mins → ⑦ Westminster Abbey.

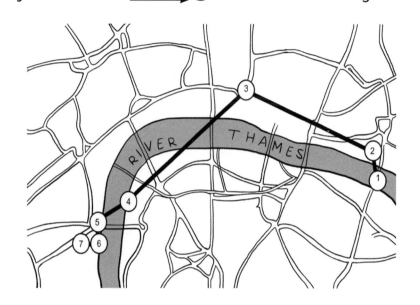

a) If you leave Tower Bridge at 1p.m. what time will you reach Big Ben? _____

b) How long will it take for you to walk from the Tower Bridge to Westminster Palace? _____

c) How long will it take you to walk from Westminster Palace to The Tower of London? _____

17 **Write down two questions involving travelling time using this map. Let your partner solve them and check the answers.**

_____

_____

18 Read the clues. Colour the picture correctly.

James is the tallest. He has brown hair and he is wearing a red shirt. His sign is yellow.

The shortest person is holding a green sign and wearing a pink shirt.

The other person has long blonde hair. This person is wearing a yellow shirt and blue skirt, and is holding a pink sign.

19 One of the learners has written you an email to ask what the weather will be like during their visit. Write a short reply telling her what to expect.

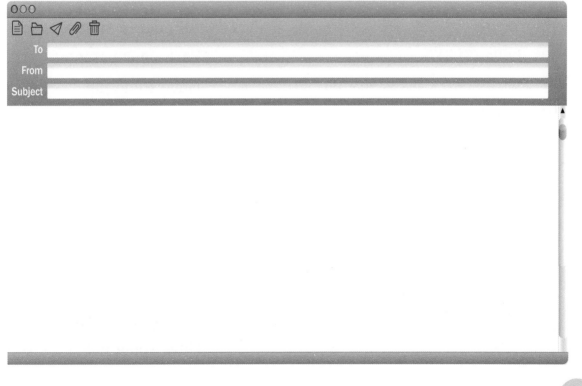

Songs and chants

Unit 9 Week 1

Audio 24

Song: *We're going to the game reserve*

Today we're going to the game reserve

The game reserve, the game reserve,

Today we're going to the game reserve

I wonder what we'll see.

Look over there – I see a lion

It's by itself, it's by itself

Look over there – I see a lion

In the game reserve.

Look down there – I see some buck

Next to the tree, next to the tree,

Look over there – I see some buck,

In the game reserve.

Look over there – I see a giraffe,

Eating some leaves, eating some leaves,

Look over there – I see a giraffe,

In the game reserve.

Look up there – I see an eagle,

Flying high, flying high,

Look over there – I see an eagle,

In the game reserve

Unit 9 Week 3

Audio 26

Chant: *We are going on a holiday*

We are going on a holiday

Where do you think we'll go?

We'll go to London to see the queen,

And also see a show.

Pack your passport

Have some fun

Book the taxi

For everyone!

We are going on a holiday

Where else shall we go?

We'll go to Turkey to see some great places

All built long ago.

Pack your passport

Have some fun

Book the taxi

For everyone!

We are going on a holiday

What are we going to do?

We'll go to Switzerland and learn to ski

And build a snowman too!

Pack your passport

Have some fun

Book the taxi

For everyone!